The Church in William of Ockham

American Academy of Religion
Studies in Religion

edited by
Stephen D. Crites

Number 16
The Nature, Structure and Function
of the Church in William of Ockham
by John J. Ryan

THE NATURE, STRUCTURE AND FUNCTION OF THE CHURCH IN WILLIAM OF OCKHAM

John J. Ryan

Scholars Press

Distributed by
Scholars Press
PO Box 5207
Missoula, Montana 59806

The Nature, Structure and Function
of the Church in William of Ockham

by
John J. Ryan

BV
598
. R9

Library of Congress Cataloging in Publication Data

Ryan, John Joseph.
   The nature, structure, and function of the Church
in William of Ockham.

   (AAR studies in religion ; no. 16 ISSN 0084-6287)
   Includes bibliographical references.
   1. Church—History of doctrines—Middle Ages,
600-1500. 2. Ockham, William, d. ca. 1349. I. Title.
II. Series: American Academy of Religion. AAR
studies in religion ; no. 16.
BV598.R9   262'.001   78-2891
ISBN 0-89130-230-1 pbk.

Printed in the United States of America

1   2   3   4   5   6

Edwards Brothers, Inc.
Ann Arbor, MI 48104

CONTENTS

INTRODUCTION

The revisions of the past generation of Ockham scholarship have attempted to put William of Ockham's political writings back into a reasonably proportioned and credible fourteenth-century setting. It never really was historically plausible that Ockham, the erudite and reclusive Franciscan theologian, should have been an advocate of Marsilius of Padua's secularizing radicalism. His invitation to the prince to assume his rightful power with regard to the Church never looked forward to the Erastian future but backward to the never-never world of the idealized imperial past. More naive than radical, more academically remorseless than prophetic in the application of his thought, Ockham anticipated neither the Scriptural insights nor the revolutionary reconception of the nature of Christianity to qualify him as a fore-runner of the Reformation. Indeed, twentieth century scholarship stops just short of implying that, given the intellectual and social climate, Ockham's thought is just about what one ought to have expected of an acute and learned theologian of his day. His philosophical nominalism is now seen as grossly misunderstood and its connection with his doctrine of the Church gratuitously imputed, either by the ill will of theological opponents or the gleeful co-optation of Protestant polemicists. He was fundamentally an orthodox Catholic believer, it is now said, who was led by unfortunate circumstances into opposition to the pope. If his positions were sometimes insubordinate and unnecessarily contentious they were not, for all that, heretical.[1]

Much of course depends upon what meaning is given to the word 'heretical': whether Ockham is to be judged by the canons of a later time or by the unarticulated orthodoxy of his own. If the standards of Trent are applied, it is said, then of course Ockham's orthodoxy looks doubtful. But if he is judged by the rather more fluid norms of the late-Middle Ages, and compared especially to such firebrands as Marsilius and Wyclif, he will reappear as he really was, a curmudgeon perhaps, but a fundamentally orthodox curmudgeon. If he was scandalously rebellious and spoke violently of the pope, it must be remembered that the papacy during the Avignonese period did not have nearly so secure and unchallengable a doctrinal or moral authority as once it had and was to have again.

Most of this is true, and yet it does not make the prevailing position on Ockham much more satisfactory than the older, its failure being that it does not do justice to the really revolutionary side of Ockham. Backward-looking, bookish traditionalist that he was in political and social thinking,[2] and doctrinally even something of a conservative, his theoretical treatment of the Church's structure and life is bold almost to the point of a recklessness which belies his formal, if rather nominal, acceptance of the orthodox medieval doctrine of the Church. Indeed the special interest of his ecclesiology is the schizophrenic tension between the formally orthodox elements in his theory of the Church and departures and adjustments which are cut to no earlier medieval pattern and are quite peculiarly his own.

It will be the object of this work to set that tension out in all its dimensions as clearly as possible, to exhibit the traditionalism of Ockham's formal professions about the Church and, in contrast, the radicalism of his treatment of the principles he sets for the Church's actual functioning.

Not much in the nature of biographical detail is necessary to our purpose. As a matter of fact the life of Ockham is shadowed in a rather surprising amount of obscurity, considering the celebrity, or notoriety, he enjoyed even in his own time. We are not sure of the year of his birth (probably between 1280 and 1285 at Ockham in Surrey), or how and when he became a Franciscan, or when he came to Oxford, or exactly why he had not yet achieved his doctorate at the time of his summoning to Avignon.[3] We know that through the intrigues of the former chancellor of Oxford, who apparently took serious exception to William's teaching career there, he was 'delated' in 1323 to the papal court at Avignon on the charge of dangerous, erroneous, heretical teaching in connection with his writings on the Eucharist. There he remained for four years, from 1324 to 1328,[4] in detention (probably at the Franciscan cloister there) while his case was protracted, postponed, and finally decided against him. And again, the obscurity: we do not know why there was no subsequent papal action, or why he had to remain beyond the 1326 recommendation for the condemnation of fifty-one propositions drawn from his writings.[5] We only know that he was still there when the Franciscan Minister General, Michael of Cesena, was himself summoned to Avignon to answer charges of intrigue against John XXII, arriving in December of 1327.

Ockham himself tells us that his troubles with the Curia were not the reason for his break with Avignon, that he was still an obedient subject, until upon the order of Michael, he set himself to study (for the first time, he tells us) the pronouncements of Pope John on Franciscan poverty.[6]

Upon his accession to the papal throne in 1317 John XXII had determined to settle the dispute which had been raging for decades in the Franciscan Order between those (called Spirituals) who advocated a strict observance of the evangelical ideal of poverty as practiced by St. Francis and the main body of the Order who were relatively content with the relaxing accommodations written into the Rule and accumulated in the ongoing practice of Franciscan life. Having moved almost at once against the Spirituals, sometime after 1320 he decided to condemn their teachings;[7] but the successive papal bulls accomplishing this end went well beyond the Spirituals' positions into the heart of the general Franciscan understanding of evangelical poverty. These bulls of 1322-23 were regarded throughout the Order as a repudiation of Franciscan poverty and, by some, even of that poverty taught by Christ and the Apostles.

Though there is nothing to suggest that Ockham had ever belonged to the party of the Spirituals, what he read in those bulls, he tells us, scandalized and shocked him. Forthwith he decided that John was a heretic and no true pope. We find him thereupon joining the Minister General's revolt and flight from Avignon.

Under the cover of night, on May 26, 1328, William took ship with the head of the Franciscans and a small party of the brethren down the Rhone to Aigues-Mortes, where they were met by a galley which may have been sent by the emperor Lewis of Bavaria, with whose open opposition to Pope John, the Pope himself believed Michael to be secretly in league. The rebels were conveyed to Pisa, where they awaited the arrival of Lewis, who had recently installed an anti-pope at Rome to administer his own coronation as Holy Roman Emperor. Lewis was in fact in ignominious retreat from central Italy but determined to pursue his enemies until he heard on January 13, 1330 of the death of his rival for the imperial throne, Frederick of Austria. Thereupon with the dissident Minorites in his entourage, he crossed the Alps to Germany and in February 1330 arrived in Munich. There William was to spend the rest of his life,[8] practically all of his literary work being devoted at least indirectly to the cause of the Bavarian, and to polemical treatises on the Church and the abusive and tyrannical excesses of the Avignonese papacy.

This corpus of polemical writings constitutes the source for almost everything which can be said about Ockham's theory of the Church.[9] There are almost no explicit ecclesiological considerations in the earlier theological and philosophical writings, and none, of course, in the few contemporary logical treatises. But it is far from constituting anything approaching a systematic or constructive treatment of the Church. It cannot be characterized simply as either theological or political, nor does it concern itself only with the church-state problem. Its thirteen separate writings detail matters of belief, church-polity, the origins of ecclesial and political authority, the criteria for authentic teaching and for obstinate heresy, etc. But from it we can gather an unmistakably individual and radical theology of the Church which, however, testifies to the transitional nature of the era in which it was produced.

It cannot be said that Ockham's ecclesiological thinking shows a steady movement further and further into extreme positions. Rather, from the first extant polemical work which is undoubtedly his, the *Opus nonaginta dierum*,[10] characteristics which mark his ecclesiology as faithful to the preceding medieval tradition are juxtaposed with others which indicate a definite departure from that tradition. Ockham accepts the structure of the Church as divinely instituted while interpreting institutional function in anything but a traditional way. He shifts the emphasis from structural to personal prerogatives, from the regular to the exceptional situation, from the rights of the teaching office to those of the believer. Most prominently he denies infallibility to any Church office, structure, or individual while yet locating it (in his own special interpretation of it) within the Church. The bifurcation apparent in these disparate tendencies remained a consistent characteristic throughout the polemical corpus.

Our procedure will be first to show wherein Ockham is traditional and wherein and how he departs from the tradition. We shall try to show the principles at work in what can only be called a strategy of dissociation of the Church from its structures. After that we shall try to illuminate the dynamic at work in this dissociation. Finally we shall try to decide if Ockham's ecclesiology works as a coherent theory.

[1]P. Boehner, O.F.M., *Collected Articles on Ockham*, ed. by Eligius m. Buytaert (Philosophy Series, No. 12; St. Bonaventure, N.Y.: Franciscan Institute Publications, 1958). Hereinafter referred to as *Collected Articles*. Léon Baudry, *Guillaume D'Occam: sa vie, ses oeuvres, ses idées sociales et politique*, Vol. I: *L'Homme et les oeuvres* (Paris: Libraire Philosophique J. Vrin, 1950). The second volume was never written. Hereinafter cited as *Vie*. John B. Morrall, "Some Notes on a Recent Interpretation of William of Ockham's Political Philosophy," *Franciscan Studies*, IX (December, 1949), 335-69. Wilhelm Kölmel, *Wilhelm Ockham und seine kirchenpolitischen Schriften* (Essen: Ludgerus Verlag Hubert Wingen Kg., 1962). Robert Guelluy, *Philosophie et théologie chez Giullaume d'Ockham* (Louvain: E. Nauwelaerts, 1947). Sebastien Day, *Intuitive Cognition: A Key to the Significance of the Later Scholastics* (Franciscan Institute Publications, No. 4; St. Bonaventure, N.Y.: Franciscan Institute, 1947). A virtually complete account of this newer research in Helmar Junghams, *Ockham im Lichte der neuren Forschung (Arbeiten zur Geschichte und Theologie des Luthertums*, Vol. XXI; Berlin: Lutherisches Verlagshaus, 1968). Since the publication of the latter: Jürgen Miethke, *Ockhams Weg zur Sozialphilosophie* (Berlin: Walter De Gruyter and Company, 1969). Arthur Stephen McGrade, *The Political Thought of William of Ockham: Personal and Institutional Principles* (Cambridge: Cambridge University Press, 1974). Gordon Leff, *William of Ockham: The Metamorphosis of Scholastic Discourse* (Manchester: Manchester University Press, 1975).

[2]Since this was first written Arthur Stephen McGrade's excellent, perceptive, and judicious study, *The Political Thought of William of Ockham. Personal and Institutional Principles* (Cambridge: Cambridge University Press, 1974) has appeared. McGrade shows that Ockham has used traditional principles in quite novel arrangements towards practical political positions which were really unprecedented.

[3]The best biography of Ockham is still the uncompleted work of Baudry, see *above*, n. 1. Boehner also has updated biographical details in *Collected Articles*. The editors of the critical edition of Ockham's political writings, J. G. Sikes, H. S. Offler, B. L. Manning, R. F. Bennett, and R. H. Snape, *Opera politica* (3 vols.; Manchester: Manchester University Press, 1940-63), have assembled the latest biographical consensus in their several introductions to the individual writings.

[4]1324-28. See Ockham's letter to his Franciscan brethren, written to the Pentecost general chapter of 1334, *Opera politica*, III, 1-17. Baudry, *Vie*, pp. 114-16, gives the year of flight as 1328.

[5]See A. Pelzer, "Les 51 articles de Guillaume Occam censurées en Avignon, en 1326," *Études l'histoire littéraire sur la scolastique médiévale* (Louvain: Publications universitaires, 1964), pp. 508-19. Baudry, *Vie*, pp. 99-100.

[6]"Fere quattuor annis integris in Avinione mansi, antequam cognoscerem praesidentem ibidem pravitatem haereticam incurisse. Quia nolens leviter credere quod persona in tanto officio constituta haereses definiret esse tenendas, constitutiones haereticales ipsius nec legere nec habere curavi.," *ad fratres*, p. 6. The documents in question are *Quia nonnunquam*, March 26, 1322 (Baluze-Mansi, pp. 207-08), *Ad conditorem canonum*, December 8, 1322 (Baluze-Mansi, pp. 221-24), and *Cum inter nunnullos*, November 12, 1323 (Baluze-Mansi, p. 224).

[7]M. D. Lambert, *Franciscan Poverty* (London: S.P.C.K., 1961), pp. 218-21.

[8]He died there, probably in 1349, and is buried beside Michael of Cesena and Bonagratia of Bergamo in the choir of the Franciscan cloister. For the biographical details, Baudry, *Vie*, pp. 118-29; 232, 247.

[9]The following are the polemical works generally accepted as the genuine works of Ockham: Junghans, p. 92. The chronological sequence generally agreed upon is: *Opu nonaginta dierum* (1333), *Dialogus* I (1333-34), *Epistola ad Fratres Minores* (April, 1334), *De dogmatibus papae Johannis XXII* (1334), *Contra Joannem* (1335), *Contra Benedictum* (1337-38), *Compendium errorum papae* (1338), *An princeps pro suo succι sι* (1339), *Dialogus* III (1339-41), *Breviloquium de principatu tyrannico* (1341), *Octo quaestiones de potestate papae* (1342), *Consultatio in causa matrimoniali* (near beginning of 1342), *De imperatorum et pontificum potestate* (1346-47). See Baudry, *Vie*, pp. 151-232, *passim*. This list does not include the *Allegationes de potestate imperiali* (1338) or the *Quia saepe iuris* (*De electione Caroli*) (1348) among the genuine writings. Sikes, "Introduction" to *Opus*, p. 290, puts the *Opus* in 1332, as does Jurgen Miethke, *Ockhams Weg*, p. 83. The latter puts the *Octo quaestiones* in 1341, before the *Breviloquium*, which he situates in 1341-42, ibid., p. 115.

[10]*Opus nonaginta dierum*, Vols. I and II of *Opera politica*. (This work straddles Volumes I and II but is paginated consecutively.) Hereinafter referred to as *Opus*. It is not without significance that it was written as a public defense of the whole Michaelist party and may include subsidiary considerations which are not specifically Ockham's own opinions or concerns.

1 THE DISENGAGEMENT OF THE CHURCH FROM ITS STRUCTURES

Ockham remained faithful to the orthodox belief that office in the Church—and office as the medieval Church had long conceived it—is of divine institution and not of human origin. This holds in the first place for the papacy. In the *Breviloquium*, one of the later works, he writes:

> The pope has some power from the divine law and immediately from the ordination of Christ, such as the power of Order and the power of teaching, and that of demanding temporal goods because of the spiritual things which he sows in the people.[1]

Ockham seldom mentions the power "que ordinis est," the power given by Christ in the sacrament of Order validly to administer the Eucharist and the other sacraments. And in that very fact is ample evidence that he found nothing fundamental to dispute in the sacramental system as a whole. He accepts and even takes for granted the orthodox belief that, given the required conditions, the sacraments are divinely empowered with an inviolable inner efficacy of grace. He further holds that the power to administer the Eucharist, absolution from sins, and the sacrament of Order is a divine power bestowed in the latter sacrament by Christ upon the priesthood.[2]

His major concern is for that other power, traditionally called the "power of jurisdiction," which is described in the passage above as "the power of teaching, and that of demanding temporal goods." This power the pope has because it was given by Christ to Peter.[3] Peter was given preeminent authority in the Church, having himself directly received the keys; and as vicar of Christ he has received all the power which Christ as mortal man had over his followers as their leader.[4] There is no doubt that in a special sense (surpassing, that is, the sanction of any legitimate worldly authority) the authority of Peter and his successors is more than human:

> But the sanction or definition of the Roman pontiff, if it has been correct, especially as regards faith, must be so accepted as confirmed by the divine voice of blessed Peter.[5]

There is also no doubt that for Ockham the papal office is not only the highest office in the Church by the institution of Christ: it is ruler of all the rest and, unless its holder is guilty of heresy or obdurate wrongdoing, answerable to no one under God. Examples of how literally he takes the papal primacy are such statements as: 1)"The whole multitude of the faithful except the pope is beneath the pope,"[6] and 2)"A pope who is not incorrigible is judged by the

Lord only."[7] The last is, indeed, a canonical commonplace. The pope is the vicar of Christ, not the delegate of the Church. Those who try to see Ockham as basically an early proponent of democratic government in the Church are, in regard to his fundamental thinking, clearly mistaken.[8] The authority which is proper to the Church is regularly from above, not below.

The episcopal office, too, originates from above, in divine institution. Ockham shows no hesitation in ascribing apostolic origin to the episcopal office, as Christ himself instituted the office of the apostles:

> For although prelates in some ways hold the place of the apostles, namely as to spiritual jurisdiction; and the preaching of the Gospel and the dispensing of the sacraments. . .[9]

He regularly associates bishops and prelates with the apostles as ruling in the name of Christ:

> to whom thus the governing of the faithful principally belongs on the earth.[10]

> . . .since he [i.e. the prelate] ought to preach those things to others, according to the command of Christ, who said to the apostles, as the last chapter of Matthew has it: *Teach them, that is all nations, to observe whatever I have commanded you.* . . . Among which, however, is the command to obey their prelates.[11]

The authority of bishops is thus to be granted a divine origin also.

To this extent we have in Ockham a traditional 'Catholic' view of apostolic succession. The offices of pope and bishop in the Church are an institution of Christ, the authority of bishops stemming ultimately from the apostles, whose successors they are, legally as well as historically.[12] This belief in the apostolic succession of bishops explains Ockham's acceptance of the Roman church's claim to be the successor to the authority of Peter, though its place is owing to the decision of Peter, not to any ordination of Christ.[13]

Ockham's doctrine of the Church as both sacrament-bearer and authority-bearer is recognizably the common doctrine of the Middle Ages. It is only when he comes to theorize upon this doctrinal foundation that we see what he is actually up to in his treatment of the Church.

Ockham's departures from tradition

What is distinctive about Ockham's treatment of Church office is that, while everywhere acknowledging the traditional conceptions, he is uncomfortable with them and refuses to use them as constructive principles in his ecclesiological thinking. The reason, at least one reason, is not far to seek: to allow office an ultimate and unconditional validity, or even that validity which had become the medieval tradition before him would be to contradict his experience of the Avignon papacy. He cannot or will not deny the divine origin of office in the Church. He must therefore relativize its authority; he must limit, qualify, and condition. In the sustained, relentless way he pursues these restrictions there clearly emerges a more or less conscious attempt to disengage the Church from its structure of offices. In what follows we shall examine his relativizing strategies and the principles undergirding them to determine how he sees office and structure in their relationship to the Church's essential reality.

Relativization of the papal office

The most pervasive principle at work in Ockham's polemical writings, calling forth their most persistent themes, is that all power given by God to men is limited. It is thus distinctive of Ockham to treat the papal office more in terms of its limits than of its prerogatives, and about these limits he is not only explicit but shrill.

Christ gave "certain limits" to Peter's power, which should not be transgressed.[14] If there were no limits to Peter's power, and thus the pope's, he would have received all the power of Christ himself and would have been able to institute new sacraments, dispense from those we have, change the divine law, etc.[15] The pope, being a mortal and imperfect man, cannot have all the power which Christ, even as mortal man, possessed. The pope's power, whatever its extent, is not and can not be literally 'divine,' as was Christ's. The vicar of Christ has not received a power equal to that of Christ insofar as Christ was "homo passibilis et mortalis (vulnerable and mortal man)."[16] If there were no limits to the papal power the pope could make slaves of all men, introduce obligations at his whim, transfer kingdoms at will, etc.[17] Who can consider that Christ would have given such power to a weak and sinful human being?[18]

> It would not have been expedient for the Christian people that he should give such power to his vicar.[19]

As a consequence of this conviction Ockham takes perhaps his most insistent position, that against the teaching of a papal plenitude of power in the spiritual and temporal spheres. Of course his opposition to a temporal plenitude of power is not particularly noteworthy, since by his time it appears to have been—except at the curia—the majority position. Even in the spiritual sphere he does not precisely deny that there is a kind of papal plenitude of power which can be spoken of; indeed he uses the term himself:

> The supreme pontiff, as regards ecclesiastical rule and power, obtains a plenitude of power.[20]

Rather, one might say, he qualifies the plenitude out of existence. His first extended attack upon the curialist doctrine of the papal plenitude, i.e., that the pope has the power to do or command anything which is not forbidden by the divine or natural law, occurs in the *Tractatus contra Benedictum*. There, in specifically rejecting that contention, he denies that the pope can impose arbitrary burdens either in matters purely of cult or other "spiritual" things, not to speak of "temporal or servile" matters.[21] In his most comprehensive polemical attack upon the papal plenitude, the *Breviloquium*, he declares that apart from questions of guilt on the part of his subjects, or of grave necessity or commensurate utility, the pope may not add any "novelties" to the evangelical law, especially such as would be grave or onerous. Thus, without the consent of the faithful he cannot regularly command any special fast or abstinence.[22]

The most explicit short statement of the scope and limits of the papal plenitude is to be found in the *Dialogus* III.[23] Here Ockham tells us that the pope cannot regularly command anything which is only of counsel and not of precept. Thus, for instance, he cannot make laws commanding Christians, individually or as a whole, either to preserve virginity or to contract marriage, to assume poverty or to retain riches, to give or not give alms. In general, he cannot command anything which faith and good morals can do without.[24] The examples, rather outrageous and certainly not representative of actual papal practice, only heighten Ockham's anxiety to nibble the idea to death. The same purpose can be observed in this passage of the *Dialogus* III, which fairly bristles with obsessive qualifications:

> Christ constituted Blessed Peter as head, chief, and prelate over the other Apostles and all the faithful. He gave him a *regular* fullness of power in spiritual matters for the purposes of *necessary* government, by deed *or omission*, of the community of the faithful in good morals or any of their spiritual necessities. This power obtains in such things as should *prudently* and *without danger* be committed to a single man for the common utility. He also gave him that liberty and coercive jurisdiction which would be without *any* detriment or notable or excessive diminution of the rights of the empire, of kings, princes, or anyone else, laity or clergy.[25] (Italics mine)

Perhaps the most fundamental theological principle undergirding the limitations and restrictions which Ockham emphasizes in the conduct of the papacy is that of Christian liberty. The occasion for his first declarations on the subject was a papal constitution imposed by Benedict XII on the Franciscan general chapter at Cahors on Pentecost, 1337,[26] which states that no one is to presume to decide a question of faith about which there are differences of opinion once that question has been presented for judgment to the Apostolic See. Ockham calls this an "unheard of temerity," "a heresy worse than all the others" which have ever been taught. Worse cannot be mentioned, since it destroys all the contents of Scripture and every article of faith by maintaining that the supreme pontiff is to be believed more than God Himself.[27]

After detailing in the next several chapters all the categories of faith-statements which every Catholic must believe explicitly no matter what question is brought before the Apostolic See, he attacks the argument that Christians must submit their faith to the correction of the pope because of his plenitude of power. He suggests that this position might well be heretical:

> Indeed to some it seems heretical to say that he can do all such things, because according
> to Scripture the Christian law is a law of liberty, and greater liberty at that than was the
> old law. But if the pope could do everything which is not against the divine and natural
> law, the Christian law would be that of the greatest slavery.[28]

Ockham reverts to this theme again and again in his later works, giving the details of his conception of Christian liberty.[29] The Christian is to be free from papal invasions not only of his temporal rights and liberties, but also of his spiritual and religious prerogatives. The evangelical inspiration of this concern is evidenced by the regular citation of New Testament passages referring to Christian liberty—Jas 1:25, Acts 15:7ff., Gal 2:3-4, 5:12-13, 2 Cor 3:17. It is an echo of the evangelical protest in the name of the apostolic life which had long found difficulty with institutional demands, and which had formed the environment out of which the mendicant Orders had sprung.[30] The Christian is free from all religious works and observances which are not commanded by the divine law and the Gospel. Apart from sin and the spiritual power to punish it, the pope may not ordinarily impose works of supererogation upon the Christian. He does not have the power to impose grave obligation when neither the divine nor the natural law nor voluntarily undertaken responsibilities impose it.[31] It is not just that the pope has limited power; it is that by the Gospel the Christian has been made free.

The role of the episcopacy

The limitations which Ockham sees in the papal office will of course hold *a fortiori* for the episcopacy, which itself has further limitations. Ockham seldom considers the office of bishop as an individual office: his attention is drawn rather to the bishops as a collective *magisterium*, and here too he refuses to see the object of the promise of Christ:

> The college or community of archbishops and bishops can err against the faith . . .
> because Christ did not promise that the Catholic faith would endure in bishops until the
> end.[32]

The passage begins by speaking of a "college," a "community," and ends, significantly, with a mere plurality, in accordance with Ockham's habit of treating wholes as not other than the sum of parts. Ockham is not thinking of a structured group here (except to set this "college" over against the "college" of cardinals), but when he does advert to such a group, a council, the assembly adds no decisive reality to the multiplicity of bishops.

> Those persons who, living in different places, can err against the faith, even if they
> assemble in the same place, can err against the faith, because the coming together in the
> same place does not make some people undeviating in regard to the faith. . . . But all
> who convene at a general council, before they come together, can err against the faith
> . . . therefore even after they convene, they can fall into heretical depravity.[33]

Of course, the overriding interest of this passage is its clear rejection of the infallibility of the general council.[34]

As a matter of fact, Ockham has difficulty in seeing the general council as really an organ of Church authority at all. It seems to lack any separate or irreplaceable function beyond that of emergency juridical resort and representative decision.[35] The bishops, it appears, have no inherent right as a group to assembly in council. The general council is put by Ockham in the category of occasional and emergency counsellor to the pope or to the Church as a whole.

The context for this interpretation is a discussion of whether government by several is better for the Church than government by one.[36] Ockham argues that the judgment of several can be as perverted and unwise as the judgment of one, here adapting the argument of his famous razor:

> Whenever one person suffices in such a way that he needs neither the advice nor the indulgence of others, many should not be called. For uselessly is done through many what equally well can be done through one.[37]

But sometimes, he grants, many heads may be better than one:

> Whence, if it seems probable that when some persons are called to a general council they will not celebrate the council properly, they should be prevented from assembling. If, however, it seems probable that they will celebrate the council properly, their assembling should be arranged, unless it seems that there would be less utility than inconvenience in it.[38]

How grudging he is to the idea of a council! It is surely not for him an essential organ of government. In principle it need never be convoked, because the pope may never need its advice. Only extraordinarily, even when convoked, will it be able to pass beyond advice to rule or decision.[39]

The function of the general council for Ockham is not (as is the function of office) to dispense divine things to the Church but rather to serve the Church when needed for the common utility. Whence it is the Church primarily, not the pontiff, in whose name the council is convoked.[40] In an emergency situation, if the pope is negligent in his concern for the Church, a council may be summoned without his authority.[41] Even called by the whole Church and representative of it, the council cannot bear the whole authority of that which it represents:

> A person or college who or which represents another does not enjoy every prerogative which the community it represents enjoys.[42]

The context, pointing out the limited prerogatives of a representative, acknowledges that both a general council and a pope represent the universal Church and yet both can err against the Faith. Since the universal Church is infallible this means that neither can fully represent it. The council is a human convocation, which the Church is not:

> But certain persons called together in general council are called only by human convocation, nor do they receive any authority or power except from human commission.[43]

Office in the Church, whatever its limitations, is of divine convocation, and this is the reason why ordinarily a council is not above but under a pope,[44] having, in the ordinary course, no authority over a pope in matters of Faith.[45]

Limitations on official law and teaching

The most crucial, pervasive, and typical of the principles which Ockham uses as strategies of relativization and therefore limitation upon hierarchical office in the Church is the disjunction he maintains between office and the divine prerogatives of the totality of the Church. It goes to the heart of his distinctive ecclesiology, constituting perhaps its most radical principle of function. It is expressed in his interpretation of certain crucial words of Christ. In Luke 22:32 Christ prays that the faith of his followers may not fail and in Matthew 28:20 he promises to be present with them to the end of time. Ockham interprets both prayer and promise as given only to the whole Church:

> That which is promised to the whole and to no part should not be attributed to any part, even the more important. But . . . this promise was made to no part.[46]

The principle that what applies to the whole Church must not be attributed to any part of it as such applies even (or in his concern *especially*) to the papacy:

> What applies to the whole Church must not be attributed to part of the Church, even to the principal part . . .[47]

Ockham employs this principle to deny all particular prerogatives of infallibility.[48] Since no part can enjoy the special prerogatives of the totality of the Church no part—and no office—enjoys that one either.[49]

But as applied to the regular authoritative workings of the Church the principle has two corollaries for him. The first is that even that which is divinely instituted to rule the whole (i.e., the papacy) can never have the complete authority of the whole. The authority which the Church in the totality of its members possesses is not at the disposal of even the highest office in the Church, though that office has supreme authority over the whole Church. Nor is that authority of the whole to be found in the general council, which, as we have seen, only imperfectly represents the universal Church. Ockham should be taken seriously when he demands that the full authority of the Church could be present only if the whole Church could be assembled:

> Even to the universal Church, if it could assemble, appeal would principally have to be made.[50]

Really it is only this universal Church of the living which has succeeded to the apostolic Church, only this Church of everyone which can "represent" the Church.[51]

The second corollary is that official teaching, like Church law, is always subject to the judgment of the universal Church. The pope's definitions must always be measured against other and surer norms.[52] Because he can err and incur "heretical depravity" his definitions are to be accepted only if they are correct and consonant with orthodox faith.[53] Thus it can happen that a pope is summoned, when reasonably suspect of heresy, to the judgment of the Church, and to this extent the pope can have a superior in questions of Faith:

> The second error . . . is that one cannot appeal lawfully from the pope. The third . . . is that in a question of faith the pope does not have any earthly superior.[54]

That the pope in a question of heresy has a superior judge was a statement in Gratian's *Decretum* which had begun a long course of canonistic speculation about what should be done if the pope were to fall into heresy and what were the situations in which the pope would be accountable to the judgment of the Church in the name of its general welfare.[55] The background for this speculation was the fact, admitted on all sides, that some past popes had actually fallen into heresy. There had to be some way for the Church to protect itself against this contingency. The way chosen was the general council. Ockham is on solidly traditional ground, and knows it, in adducing one of the most famous canonical principles relevant to the case:

> Where it is a question of faith, the synod is greater than the pope (glossa, di. XIX, c. Anastasius).[56]

To be sure, he does not mean, as the later conciliarists did, that the pope regularly has an official, institutional superior in matters of faith. He is speaking in the context of a question, a reasonable doubt about the pope's faith. The general council is invoked as judge not because of its own inherent faith-prerogative (it has none, as we have seen), but because the council is the only practical way to summon the pope to the judgment of the universal Church. However deficient its representative capacities, it is the only representative of the whole Church apart from the pope,[57] and must function in the case of his defection. Its function then is not to pronounce the Faith but to correct and convert the pope.

> To the general council it also pertains to correct and convert the pope in matters of faith.[58]

Thus the authority of the general council to pass judgment is a legal authority, only imperfectly representing the authority of the universal Church and not stemming from any conciliar infallibility.

For this reason its teaching, like that of the pope, is subject to the judgment of the universal Church. Ultimately every truth must prove itself Catholic by being accepted without contradiction by *every Catholic!*

This happens, however, whenever some Catholic truths are publicly asserted and preached throughout all catholic regions and published among all catholic peoples as catholic truths, and no catholic is found who would resist such an assertion.[59]

One is tempted to wonder whether Ockham is serious about this absurd and impossible condition, which surely could never have been fulfilled in regard to any truth at any time, as he himself had to realize. He is of course capable of less extreme statements of it:

But the Catholic *peoples* agree with the foregoing prelates and doctors in the same assertion, because no Catholic *people* has been found which would contradict them. Therefore this assertion must be attributed to the universal Church and consequently must be firmly held.[60] (Italics mine)

His basic positions dictate some such consequence, since the whole of the Church cannot be less than the sum of its parts, however one thinks of the parts. He himself can regularly think of each individual believer as a constitutive and decisive part. In a discussion of the believers' response to a doctrinal promulgation there appears one of the two or three most famous of his statements:

If only one should dissent, such a truth should not be accepted.[61]

This statement has significance for other areas of Ockham's conception of the Church, as will be seen below;[62] but in this context a more extreme declaration of the accountability of official teaching could scarcely be devised.

Ockham specifies the validity of official teaching in a significant way:

For it happens that the duty of defining anything by authority of office, and thus of defining what is a heretical assertion and what is catholic belongs to the supreme pontiff and the general council.[63]

Here, as in so many points of his text, he seems to be saying something very traditional and unexceptionable—were one not already aware that his use of ordinary language like "authority," "office," and "general council" is very special indeed. As a matter of fact the phrase "defining anything by authority of office (aliquid diffinire auctoritate officii)" announces a distinction which van Leeuwen thinks "exerted a profound influence over the theology of the fourteenth and fifteenth centuries,"[64] the distinction between "authentic" or authoritative and doctrinal definitions. For Ockham the definitions of Faith promulgated by pope and council, when orthodox, are lawful, authoritative, binding upon all. When there are no good grounds for doubting or opposing them, they must be obeyed and acted upon in all external ways. Canonical sanctions can be invoked by bishops and inquisitors against those who disobey.[65] Such definitions have the effect of authoritatively terminating all public discussion and controversy:

No one is permitted publicly to support and knowingly to hold the contrary.[66]

But the important point is that such definitions *cannot of themselves command the inner assent of faith.* Their faith-authority comes to them only from the universal belief of the Church which they are presumed to reflect. If there is reasonable doubt that they do reflect this belief assent may inwardly be refused. When they are clearly opposed to that belief they must be openly combatted by whoever sees them to be so opposed.[67] The value of such definitions in the best of cases is thus primarily authoritative rather than doctrinal; as doctrine they are submitted to a more ultimate authority. Indeed we will now see that there is a better norm of that ultimate authority than official teaching in the Church.

The authority of doctors

Another way of "defining," with a different kind of authority, is "per modum doctrinae," the doctrinal explanations of the learned:

> Sometimes definition happens in a doctrinal way, whereby the Masters in the schools define and determine questions.[68]

> The pope is not permitted to interpret the words of God and Christ in any other way than others interpret them, nor is he more to be believed in such matters than another wise man. Indeed in such matters those more expert than the pope should be preferred to the pope himself.[69]

The teaching of the pope is thus regularly to be submitted to the judgment of theologians, and not only that of the pope but of the councils as well:

> If some assertion . . . even of general councils . . . be in no way opposed to theology, . . . it ought not to be reckoned among the heresies.[70]

This casual way of subjecting councils to theology (instead of the other way around) is of course not through the agency of the prelates of the Church. Those who "define" doctrinally (though not of course infallibly) are rather the theologians, the doctors, "those who treat of the divine Scripture."[71] Ockham entertained no small view of the prerogatives of at least his own expertise. For Ockham doctors have a status in the Church almost amounting to office—he mentions their "jurisdiction."[72] From ancient times, he tells us, doctors have been preferred to prelates in doctrine[73] and that Gratian himself

> likens in a general way the status of doctors to that of bishops.[74]

In view of the broadness of the claim, it would be inaccurate to see here the unacknowledged and persecuted expert salving his self-esteem. The office of doctor itself is plainly important to Ockham, and this seems to be the reason why in quoting Gratian's remarks about doctors he omits the latter's qualification to the acceptance of their authority: "If they should excel (si . . . preemineant)." Doctors should be preferred to bishops in matters of doctrine, as long as they are excellent in doctrine and praiseworthy in life.[75]

In this matter of doctors, it might seem at first sight that Ockham is acknowledging another office in the Church rather than dissociating all office from the universal Church's authority. But the claim of doctors is not official but personal and circumstantial in nature, as becomes clear when he pushes the same point of view to its end and says that to judge official teaching one need not be a recognized doctor or theologian at all: one need only *know*, have the requisite knowledge. He comes very close to saying that any Catholic who considers himself adequately trained in sacred doctrine can judge on matters of Faith for himself:

> There is therefore a judgment of certain and truthful knowledge by which each person judges well concerning that which he knows, and that judgment pertains to whoever is skilled in any art . . . In the Church militant that certain judgment exists as far as concerns those things which it is necessary to believe explicitly. . . . because until the end of the world there will always be some Catholics who will explicitly in this fashion endure in the true faith.[76]

Here he has assimilated theological knowledge to the promise of Christ, leaving the implication either that the promise was made to the theologically expert—a position he consistently repudiates[77]—or that any believer sufficiently informed about a particular belief is in a position to judge for himself. The latter is confirmed by an unequivocal statement:

> But if the interpretation of the Pope should be erroneous and not consonant with the truth, it would be permitted to anyone at all who knows it is not consonant with the truth openly and publicly to condemn it.[78]

Slight indeed is the distance between this position and that of private interpretation of Scripture. A difference, of course, is that the basis of judgment is not solely the text of Sacred Scripture,[79] and thus the judgment, borne up by tradition, is not quite private. Nonetheless the independence it advocates from the Church's magisterium and the judgment of the latter it defends is recognizably a kind of private interpretation. It would be difficult to think of another theologian of his time who held such a position.[80]

Accountability of faith is Ockham's foundation for an accountability of office to the whole Church in all things, despite the fact that for him office does not derive from the Church and is not in principle answerable to it.[81] He subscribes quite explicitly to the earlier canonical tradition which makes the papal office accountable not only in cases of heresy but also in those of grave crime and scandal with consequent peril to the Church's fundamental welfare.[82] He does no more than report the tradition when he says that in "at least" two cases the pope may be deposed by the Church: heresy and a crime which is notorious, incorrigible, and thus scandalous to the Church.[83] For the canonists this position had been a counsel of necessity which never received a completely coherent explanation.[84] For the later conciliarists it amounted to the claim that a superior authority resided in the Church as a whole.[85] Ockham is closer to the early canonists than to the later conciliarists. The papal office is accountable not because it derives from the community of the Church or is institutionally subject to the authority of the whole but because such accountability is necessary for the common good of the Church in emergency situations. Another principle for relativization thus emerges: the needs of the common good justify interference in official prerogatives. This common good is founded in the needs of true belief, although it is never explicitly identified with the faith of the Church by Ockham. Neither does he say whether he regards crime and scandal as equivalent to heresy or false belief, though he evidently considers them critical dangers to the needs of true belief. Whatever he left unsaid, the good of true believers constituted for him the theological justification for an occasional, non-institutional intervention in the prerogatives of office-holders. When such dangers threaten the Church those who have the good of true believing at heart have the authority and responsibility *exceptionally* (*casualiter*) to intervene to judge the pope.[86] Having started from the position that occasionally (i.e. *casualiter*, and the frequency of such occasions is not restricted), and thus possibly at any time, office and authority may be called to account from below, according to circumstances, Ockham is led in fact to adopt a principle whose application has no practical limits. The superior, more ultimate value of true belief has rendered office radically questionable and provisional.

Church office may be apostolic, but in Ockham's coinage it is a devalued apostolicity in comparison with another sort. There is an interesting and revealing discussion of the subject in a refutation of the claims of the local Roman church to indefectible faith.[87] The claim had been made that the Roman church had an apostolic root and thus could not fail in faith. Ockham cooly replies that every truly Catholic church has an apostolic root, that is, the doctrine of the apostles, whether in Paris or Naples or Rome; and that any church is an apostolic see if it has this doctrine, even if the succession in authority from apostolic times had been or would be interrupted.[88] What matters is not apostolic succession but apostolic doctrine:

> . . . a church constituted in the root of an apostolic see through the successors of bishops, that is, a church holding the apostolic doctrine which the episcopal successors have ruled (even though at some time such rule had been interrupted) . . .[89]

Here at last Ockham uncovers for us his deepest conviction about the Church: that faith is its central meaning and task. It is faith which makes a Church apostolic: it is faith which makes a church.

A very different principle of authority breathes in these words, a striking anticipation of Luther's principle of evangelical authority. Luther will say that it is the Word of God which must rule in the Church, the true warrant of whose authority is the preaching of the Word.[90] For Ockham too faith determines the true functioning of authority in the Church.

This being so, the distinction of function between clergy and laity fades before the demands of the common good. An interesting application of this attitude occurs in a passage discussing the election of prelates.[91] Election does not pertain to the clergy specially by reason of the power of Order or their office, but because the common good of the Church will usually dictate that the clergy, as ordinarily wiser and better, deal with these matters.[92] But whenever such is not the case, the laity, who have an equal responsibility for the common good, have the same right to elect.[93] Responsibility for the common good of the Church is not apportioned by share in office or in Order. It belongs to all members of the Church by virtue of their true faith.

Another interesting aspect of this discussion is the approach it makes to the explanation of the deliberative procedures of the Church as *representative*. Certain designated persons should act for all, not just in their own name: and when they do so they bear representatively the authority of all. The only real value of a general council for Ockham is in its representative possibilities. Those who attend the council are in important respects the representatives of all in the Christian community. Therefore the laity, though they may delegate their right to others, cannot be excluded from the council:

> And nevertheless it stands in the power of the laity to involve themselves in general councils. But even if they give representative authority tacitly or expressly to the clergy, they ought in no way to be barred. . . . The clergy cannot by right exclude them.

Part, at least, of what is done in the general council by the clergy is done by commission and delegation from the laity, who have an inalienable right to attend.[94] Now the importance of this representative aspect of the general council is that it indicates how far Ockham regards the common good of the Church as a lay as well as clerical concern. Office in the Church for Ockham is from God, and spiritual authority is not representative. But when the common good is at stake, all have rights, whether or not they hold office.

> What affects all ought to be treated and approved by all, as is noted in *Gloss, di. 96, c. ubinam*. . . . But those matters which are treated in the general council affect all; because the general council ought to treat of the faith and of other things which may pertain to all Christians. Therefore the laity, whom the general council affects, can licitly be involved, if they should want to be.[95]

The common good of the Church, usually specified as the needs of the true faith, is the most generalized principle under which Ockham pursues the disengagement of the inner reality of the Church from its structures. Whatever is for the Church's good; and whatever persons or arrangements are required to accomplish it bear legitimate authority, if only for the moment, even laity over clergy:

> Wherever ecclesiastical power fails, the laity have jurisdiction within the Church, that is, over the clergy.[96]

It is a question of jurisdiction, not just of some sort of emergency permission in a circumstantial necessity. This extra-official action is legal, authoritatively carrying on the Church's public life. The only ultimate ground of Church function is the common good, transcending the sacredness of office and rendering any exercise of it provisional.

Relativization of the Church's constitution

Not only office in the Church is provisional. The very constitution of the Church, divinely established as it is, must bend to the necessities of the common good. The most daring of Ockham's positions on Church polity is that even the Christ-given constitution must obey a higher divine law. On a few occasions Ockham appeals not *to* the Church's constitution but *from* it:

> Princes and laity in many cases have power over the clergy and over a heretical pope apart from the constitution of the Church, and not only through that constitution; but they occcasionally obtain such power from the divine law.[97]

The laity's "divine right" and "power" are set over against the Church's constitution as a higher right and power coming from God. It now becomes clear that the Church's constitution is not one with her inmost nature, that the two are in principle separable.

Lest this position be deemed a disingenuous strategy for countering overweening papal power, it should be noted that Ockham grants even to the pope the power occasionally to dispense from the "general state" of the Church. The instance he mentions is the conceivable necessity for the pope to designate his own successor because of a need to protect the Church from heresy when there would be danger in delay, etc.[98] In necessity the pope can dispense even with what Scripture says, explicitly or implicitly, so long as he would not be contradicting the Faith.[99] The constitution is dispensed with by Church office itself. In other words, the departure from the constitution is not to be performed in terms of some external principle of order, some counter-constitution invalidating Church office. The Church harbors within itself the power of its own reformulation, structural reconstitution, should this be necessary; and the power stems from the will of Christ. Christ did not intend to constrain the life of the Church in the face of necessity, and one must attend not only to what Christ said but what He meant. For instance, the Church does not always have to be ruled by a pope:

> [Christ] did not totally oblige his Church to the best kind of government without its being able in a case of manifest necessity or utility to alter or omit its mode of ruling, that is, by electing no one or electing many, if doing so would manifestly help the community of the faithful, or if it were to be forced to do something like this.[100]

Many popes! There could scarcely be a more arresting example of how thoroughly contingent Ockham thinks the arrangements Christ intended for the Church. There is nothing of mystical inevitability or theological necessity in the figure and office of the pope. Even the Church must share in the radical contingency of creation.[101] From the point of view of Scriptural evidence this sort of assertion is, of course, groundless but it is deeply indicative of how casually Ockham can think of the institutional Church in contrast to really important matters of faith.

Ockham finds in the actual history of the Church exceptions to the best mode of government, specifically in those times when there was a prolonged vacancy in the papal office.[102] The example is limp and unconvincing: such vacancies, he admits, were only a matter of a few years. He is converting a fact, a state of affairs of no great consequence, into a might or, in certain circumstances, an ought. By doing so he shows a basic tendency to convert every positive enactment in the Church's life, even those by Christ himself, into a provisional arrangement, confinement to which might at any time be an inadmissible restriction on the Church's activity and needs. Hence he must elevate even the inconsequential fact of papal vacancies, *in toto* a minute fraction of the Church's duration, to the level of an available operational principle for relevant contingencies:

> Although Christ had ordained that all the faithful should obey one supreme pontiff, nevertheless, because that ordination of Christ was affirmative, not negative, it surely obliges always but not for every moment, and thus it is not necessary that all the faithful obey one pope all the time . . . and although all the faithful ought to be always ready in terms of time and place and propriety to obey a supreme pontiff, nonetheless the election of a supreme pontiff . . . can be deferred . . . up to a hundred or two hundred years, or more.[103]

The example is labored almost beyond the limits of sobriety. Ockham invokes the legal maxim that an affirmative obligation does not bind for each and every moment to arrive at the position that it need not bind for two hundred years or more! He is apparently unable to put Christ's words concerning the structure of the Church on anything approaching the level of the truths of Faith. The latter are unconditional, as faith needs no confirmation by reason. But the structure of the Church is an object of faith only in a markedly diminished way.

His position presents a curious anomaly of which he seems never to have been aware. He accepts the institutional Church as a given in the history of revelation and salvation but refuses it the status of object of faith. Somehow at this level he cannot believe *in* the Church. If it is to command the obedience of his faith it must be disengaged in whatever way is possible from dependence on its institutional functions. His relativizations and dissociations of official functioning from the Church's ultimate being and action are his attempt to preserve if not to justify his belief in the Church as a divine reality.

[1]"Papa aliquam habet protestatem ex jure divino et immediate ex ordinatione Christi sicut illam que ordinis est et potestatem docendi et potestatem exigendi temporalia propter spiritualia que seminat in populo Dei," *Brev.*, Bk. I, ch. vii, p. 47.

[2]"Actus ordinis . . . videtur esse potestas quaedam . . . actus conficiendi corpus Christi, clericos ordinandi . . . ligandi et solvendi." *Octo*, Q. I, p. 20. Also *Opus, Opera politica*, II, 827, 830, 855.

[3]". . . dans ei regulariter in spiritualibus quoad omnia quae propter regimen communitatis fidelium . . . sunt de necessitate facienda vel omittenda, omnem potestatem in his, quae . . . ad utilitatem communem committerentur," *Dial.* III, Tr. I, p. 786, ll. 49-52. Also *Princeps*, p. 244. At least once Ockham hints even at a view more associated with the curialist position: that the pope has a direct and immediate headship over every part of the Church. "Specialiter autem et principaliter papa, quia non potest omnia talia in omnibus partibus facere per seipsum, providere debet . . . qualiter per inferiores eo salubriter disponantur: et illa est sollicitudo omnium ecclesiarum quam papa debet habere," *De imp.*, ch. x, p. 23.

[4]". . . ad beatum Petrum, qui erat principalis congregator ecclesiarum. . . ," *Opus, Opera politica*, II, 696. ". . . clavis regni caelorum, una scilicet de illis, quae Dominus dedit Petro. . . ," ibid., 828. "Christus instituendo beatum Petrum vicarium suum, dicendo *Pasce oves meas*, omnia pertinentia ad Christum quae erant ad pascendas oves necessaria, eidem Petro commisit," ibid., 696. "Christus non decernens inter unum officium sibi commissum et aliud, beatum Petrum vicarium suum instituit, dicens: *Pasce oves meas*; ergo Christus quantum ad omne officium quod habuit inquantum homo respectu subditorum suorum, beatum Petrum vicarium suum instituit," ibid., 686.

[5]"Sed sanctio seu definitio Romani pontificis, si recta fuerit, praecipue circa fidem, sic accipienda est, tamquam divina voce beati Petri firmata," *C. Joann.*, p. 106.

[6]"Tota fidelium multitudo praeter papam est inferior papa. . . ," *Dial.* I, p. 477, l. 57.

[7]"Papa autem, qui non est incorrigibilis, a Domino solo iudicatur," ibid., p. 568, l. 34.

[8]E.g., R. Seeberg, *Textbook of the History of Doctrines*, trans. by C. Hay (Grand Rapids, Michigan: Baker, 1952), II, 167: "The discussion is regulated by the transfer of the idea of popular sovereignty to the Church."

[9]"Nam licet praelati quantum ad aliquid teneant locum apostolorum, scilicet quantum ad iurisdictionem spiritualem et praedicationem Evangelii et dispensationem sacramentorum. . . ," *Opus, Opera politica*, II, 823.

[10]". . . ad quos tunc principaliter in terris gubernatio spectabat fidelium," *Opus, Opera politica*, I, 356.

[11]". . . cum illas debeat aliis predicare, precipiente Christo qui dixit apostolis, ut habetur Mt. ultimo: *Docete eos, scilicet omnes gentes, servare omnis quaecunque mandavi vobis.* Inter illa autem continetur quod debeant obedire praelatis suis," *Brev.*, Bk. I, ch. v, p. 46.

[12]Köhler, p. 62, is wrong in saying "Allerdings betrachtet Occam das Papsttum nicht als eine Institution des gottlichen Rechts," as well as in using Ockham's statement "Sed Papa est minor ecclesia universali, sicut orbis maior est urbe" (*Dial.* I, p. 517, l. 15) to infer that the papal office is not supreme over the Church. On the contrary, as we have just seen, Ockham maintains that it is. The statement Köhler adduces is from a context in which Ockham is discussing a pope accused of heresy, which is for him a situation quite different from that of the proper exercise of office.

[13]*Dial.* I, pp. 488-89.

[14]"Potestati suae [i.e., Petri] certos fines, ques non deberet transgredi, assignavit. . . . Christus constituens beatum Petrum super omnes fideles, certos fines posuit, quos ei transgredi non licebat," *De imp.*, ch. i, pp. 5, 6.

[15]*Brev.*, Bk. II, ch. xxii, p. 103.

[16]Ibid.

[17]Ibid., p. 104; ch. xxi, pp. 101, 102.

[18]Ibid., p. 103.

[19]"Non fuisset expediens populo christiano quod talem dedisset suo vicario potestatem," ibid.

[20]"Summus pontifex, quantum ad regimen & potestatem ecclesiasticam, plenitudinem obtinet potestatis," *Dial.* I, p. 499, ll. 54-55.

[21]Ibid., p. 262.

[22]*Brev.*, Bk. II, ch. xvii, p. 92. McGrade, *Political Thought*, p. 216, is hardly justified in saying, "Considered in its practical aspects and in isolation from the rest of his thought, Ockham's view of the papacy as an institution seems irreproachable by any but the most ardently curialist standards." Perhaps for a twentieth century Protestant that is true; but Aquinas, just three generations before him, would have wondered exceedingly.

[23]Tr. I, pp. 786-88.

[24]Ibid., p. 787, ll. 9-15.

[25]"Christus constituit B. Petrum caput principem & praelatum aliorum Apostolorum & universorum fidelium dans ei regulariter in spiritualibus quoad omnia quae propter regimen communitatis fidelium quantum ad bonos mores, & qualescunque necessitates spirituales fidelium sunt de necessitate facienda vel omittenda, omnem potestatem in his, quae non periculose, sed provide, & ad utilitatem communem committerentur uni homini; ac libertatem & iurisdictionem eam coactivam absque omni detrimento ac dispendio notabili & enormi iurium imperialium, regum principum, & aliorum quorumcunque; laicorum vel clericorum," ibid., p. 786, ll. 48-54. Also, *De imp.*, Bk. I, ch. viii, pp. 20-21.

[26]*C. Bened.*, p. 243.

[27]Ibid., p. 243-44, p. 245.

[28]"Immo nonnullis videtur haereticum dicere quod omnis talia possit, quia secundum scripturam lex Christiana est libertatis, et maioris libertatis quam fuerit lex vetus. Si autem papa omnia posset, quae non sunt contra legem divinam et legem naturae, lex Christiana esset maximae servptutis. . . ," ibid., p. 262.

[29]Especially, *Dial.* III, Tr. I, pp. 776-77. *Brev.*, Bk. II, ch. iii-v, pp. 56-63.

[30]Ibid., ch. iii, pp. 56-57. *Dial.* III, Tr. I, p. 776. Kolmel, "Die Mensch zwischen Ordnung und Freiheit," *Beiträge zum Berufsbewusstsein des Mittelalterlichen Menschen.*, p. 216, says "Dabei gilt in allem, was nicht vom Herrn unabdingbar festgelegt ist, das Gesetz der Normenoekonomie und der evangelischen Freiheit. . . ." He also notes a "Spannung" between evangelical freedom and the given institution, ibid., 222.

[31]*Brev.*, Bk. II, ch. v, p. 62.

[32]"Collegium aut communitas archiepiscoporum & episcoporum potest contra fidem errare . . . quia Christus non promisit, quod fides catholica esset in episcopis usque ad finem permansura," *Dial.* I, p. 478, ll. 36-38.

[33]"Illae personae, quae in diversis locis existentes possunt contra fidem errare, etiam si ad eundem locum conveniunt, poterunt contra fidem errare . . . quia concursus ad eundem locum non reddit aliquos inobliquabiles a fide . . . sed omnes ad generale concilium convenientes, antequam convenirent, poterant contra fidem errare . . . ergo etiam postquam conveniunt, poterunt labi in haereticam pravitatem," ibid., p. 495, ll. 1-7, *passim. Dial.* III, Tr. II, p. 822.

[34]Van Leeuwen, "L'Église, règle de foi," p. 286, is surely mistaken in maintaining that Ockham never affirmed and did not want to affirm that a council could err. Apart from the fact that he twice devoted considerable space and detailed, thoroughly typical argumentation to proving that a council could err, it is the only position consistent with his often-reiterated principle that what was promised to the whole cannot apply to the part, see *below*, ch. ii, pp. 67-68. Van Leeuwen's position is a consequence of another, that often Ockham does not have a settled position, pp. 267, 288. Thus he can say: "Il ne nie pas absolument l'infaillibilité du concile général et de tout magistere écclésiastique," p. 287. This is true only in the sense that in the *Dialogus*, where alone he discusses the question directly, Ockham never clearly announces his own opinion.

[35]Lagarde, "Ockham et le concile général," *Album Helen Maud Cam*, Vol. I, 2 vols.; *Etudes presentées à la Commission internationale pour l'histoire des assemblées d'états* (Louvains), XXIII (1960), 88, concurs in this judgment and quotes a passage from Ockham: "Non . . . ad principandum . . . sed ad consulendum quid facere principans teneatur," *Dial.* III, Tr. I, p. 805, l. 33.

[36]*Dial.* III, Tr. I, pp. 804-6.

[37]"Quandoque unus sufficit ita quod nec consilio nec favore indiget aliorum, non sunt vocandi plures. Quia frustra fit per plures, quod aeque bene potest fieri per unum,"ibid., p. 805, ll. 56-58.

[38]"Unde si probabiliter creditur, quando aliqui ad generale concilium convocantur, quod non rite concilium celebrabunt, impediendi sunt ne conveniant. Si autem probabiliter creditur quod rite concilium celebrabunt, agendum est ut conveniant, nisi credatur quod minus utilitatis faciant quam sit incommoditas," ibid., p. 806, ll. 2-5.

[39]Lagarde, "Ockham et le concile général," p. 88: "Le Concile n'est pas un soverain dont les avis font loi, c'est un conseiller eventuel auquel on peut avoir recours pour se tirer d'un mauvais pas." Brian Tierney, *Origins of Papal Infallibility 1150-1350* (Leiden: E. J. Brill, 1972), p. 231, seriously misrepresents this point, saying that "Ockham maintained, for instance, that a council was superior to a pope."

[40]"Concilium generale habet potestatem principaliter ab ecclesia universali, cuius vicem gerit, & cuius auctoritate principaliter convocatur; sed immediate per Papam, si est catholicus & desiderat sequi iustitiam, congregetur," *Dial.* I, p. 571, ll. 28-30.

[41]"Unde & Absque Papa congregari posset in casu . . .," ibid., l. 30; also p. 602, ll. 5-21.

[42]"Non omni praerogativa gaudet persona vel collegium, quae vel q[uod] gerit vices alterius, qua gaudet communitas, cuius vices gerit," ibid., p. 494, ll. 58-59.

[43]"Sed certae personae in generali concilio congregatae, non vocantur nisi vocatione humana, nec aliquam auctoritatem, nec potestatem accipiunt, nisi ex commissione humana,"ibid., p. 495, ll. 20-24.

[44]It is surprising at this late date that so eminent an ecclesiologist as Yves M. -J. Congar, who is obviously conversant with Ockham, could still describe him as one of the most extreme conciliarists. "Incidence Écclésiologique d'un thème de dévotion Mariale," *Mélanges de science religieuse*, VII (1950), 286.

[45]*Dial.* I, pp. 518-21.

[46]"Illud q[uod] promittitur toti & nulli parti, non debuit alicui parti attribui, etiam principaliori, Sed . . . nulli parti fuit hoc promissum," ibid., p. 489, ll. 33-35.

[47]"Quod competit toti ecclesiae, non est attribuendum parti ecclesiae, etiam principali,"ibid., p. 478, ll. 41-42.

[48]The contention of Tierney, *Origins*, pp. 205-237, that Ockham taught a doctrine of "anti-papal infallibility" is totally misguided by his confusion of the irreformability of a papal document (the *Exiit* of Nicholas III which Ockham defends throughout the *Opus nonaginta*) with a papal *prerogative* of infallibility which not only the text quoted here (among many others) but the basic structure of Ockham's ecclesiology render inconceivable.

[49]Apart from its being a misreading of Ockham, it makes no sense to speak, as Tierney, *Origins*, p. 215, has Ockham speaking, of an *inability* to err applying to the pope only in the sense that if he does err, he ceases *ipso facto* to be pope. This is only as true as to say: "The king never dies." Cf. my "Ockham's Dilemma: Tierney's Ambiguous Infallibility and Ockham's Ambiguous Church," *Journal of Ecumenical Studies*, Vol. XIII, No. 1 (Winter, 1976), pp. 37-49.

[50]"Ad ecclesiam etiam universalem, si convenire posset, esset principaliter appelandum," ibid., p. 497, l. 58.

[51]*Dial.* III, Tr. I, p. 826, l. 61-p. 827, l, 1.

[52]See my *Journal of Ecumenical Studies* article, "Ockham's Dilemma," p. 45. The pope's definitions may *happen* to present the infallible faith correctly; they are never *of themselves* infallible.

[53]*C. Joann.* p. 108.

[54]"Secundus error . . . quod a papa de jure appelari non potest. Tertius . . . quod papa in causa fidei non habet superiorem in terris," *Opus, Opera politica,* II, 856.

[55]For a detailed discussion of this canonical development, see Brian Tierney, *Conciliar Theory,* especially pp. 56-67.

[56]"Ubi de fide agitur, synodus est maior papa (glossa, di. xix, c. Anastasius)," *Opus,* Opera politica, I, 296.

[57]"Sicut concilium generale repraesentat ecclesiam universalem, & eius vices gerit; ita etiam Papa repraesentat ecclesiam universalem & eius vices gerit;" *Dial.* I, p. 494, ll. 54-56.

[58]"Ad concilium generale pertinet etiam papam in hiis quae fidei sunt corrigere et emendare," *Opus, Opera politica*, II, 851. See also *Dial.* I, p. 469, ll. 42-43: ". . . concilium generale, ad quod spectat etiam Papam emendare."

[59]"Hoc autem contingit quandocumque aliquae veritates catholicae per omnes regiones catholicorum publice asseruntur et praedicantur, et apud omnes populos catholicos tanquam catholicae divulgantur et nullus invenitur catholicus qui tali assertioni resistat," *C. Joann.* p. 67.

[60]"Praemissis autem prelatis & doctoribus in eadem assertione catholici populi consenserunt, quia nullus inventus est populus catholicus qui contradiceret eis ergo haec assertio est universali ecclesiae tribuenda, & per consequens firmiter est tenenda," *Dial.* III, Tr. I, p. 865, ll. 17-20.

[61]"Si unus solus dissentiret, non esset talis veritas acceptanda," *Dial.* I, p. 429, l. 50.

[62]Ch. iv, pp. 173-74.

[63]"Contingit enim aliquid diffinire auctoritate officii & sic diffinire, quae est assertio haeretica, quae catholica est consenda, ad summum pontificem spectat & concilium generale," *Dial.* I, p. 397, ll. 35-37.

[64]"L'Église, règle de foi," p. 277.

[65]*Dial.* I, p. 421, ll. 25-34.

[66]"Nulli licebit publice contrarium opinari & tenere scienter," *Dial.* III, Tr. I, p. 811, l. 54.

[67]Ibid., ll. 57-59.

[68]"Aliquando contingit diffinire per modum doctrinae, quo modo Magistri in scholis quaestiones diffiniunt & determinant," *Dial.* I, p. 399, ll. 37-38.

[69]"Non aliter liceret papae interpretari verba Dei et Christi quam alteri, nec magis est credendum sibi in huiusmodi quam alteri sapienti. Imo in huiusmodi sunt magis periti quam papa ipsi papae praeferendi," *Dial.* III, Tr. I, p. 811, ll. 48-50.

[70]"Si aliqua assertio. . . . etiam generalium concilium . . . theologiae nullatenus obviaret. . . non tamen deberet inter haereses computari," *Dial.* I, p. 400, ll. 17-20.

[71]Ibid., p. 454, l. 65-p. 455 (wrongly numbered 461), l. 5.

[72]Ibid.

[73]Ibid., ll. 29-30.

[74]"Comparat enim in genere statum doctorum ad statum pontificum," ibid., l. 28.1

[75]Ibid., ll. 30-31.

[76]"Est itaque iudicium certae & veridicae cognitionis, quo unus quisque bene iudicat, de quo quis noscit & illud iudicium pertinet ad quemlibet in qualibet arte peritum. . . . In ecclesia militante est certum iudicium, quantum ad ea quae necesse est credere explicite. . . quia semper usque ad finem mundi erunt aliqui catholici, qui tali modo in vera fide explicite permanebunt," ibid., p. 497, ll. 25-31.

[77]See especially ibid., p. 432, ll. 1-2; p. 497, ll. 57-61. *C. Joann.* p. 67.

[78]"Si autem interpretatio Papae esset erronea & non consona veritati, liceret cuilibet scienti eam non esse consonam veritati manifeste & publice reprobare," *Dial.* III, Tr. I, p. 811, ll. 57-59.

[79]See *below*, Ch. ii, pp. 93-96.1

[80]This is not to imply that "private interpretation" is a characteristic Reformation doctrine and that Ockham is a "forerunner" of the Reformation on this point. The major reformers held what is called the perspicuity of Scripture, i.e. that Scripture is transparent to its own Spirit-guided interpretation, not that it is "privately" interpreted. E.g., "Scripture is the 'primum principium' . . . the most readily understandable [book] which interprets itself. . . ," *An Argument in Defense of All the Articles of Dr. Martin Luther Wrongly Condemned in the Roman Bull, Works of Martin Luther* (6 vols.; Philadelphia: United Lutheran Publication House, 1915-32), III, 16. "Let this point therefore stand: that those whom the Holy Spirit has inwardly taught truly rest upon Scripture, and that Scripture indeed is self-authenticated," John Calvin, *Institutes*, I, vii, 5, trans. by Ford L. Battles, Vol. XX, The Library of Christian Classics (Philadelphia: Westminster Press, 1960). The perspicuity of Scripture did not obviate for the

Reformers the necessity for a corporate doctrinal authority in the Church. d a corporate doctrinal authority in the Church. See Calvin, *Institutes,* IV, viii, l. 9.

[81]See *above*, Ch. i, pp. 13-15.

[82]Among these canonists were Huguccio, Rufinus, Stephanus Tornacensis, and the *Glossa Palatina.* See Tierney, *Conciliar Theory*, pp. 57-67. Thirteenth-century canonists, e.g. Hostiensis, were not disposed to accept any cases beyond that of heresy as reason for the pope's deposition, because for them his deposition must be automatic according to divine law, as is the case in heresy, and not humanly initiated. Cf. Lagarde, *Critique*, pp. 246-47. Curialist theologians like Augustinus Triumphus and Alvarez Pelagius, as might be expected, also rejected all other cases except heresy, saying that a criminal pope is still pope, *ibid.*

[83]"Illi autem casus ad minus sunt duo: scilicet casus haeresis et casus in quo crimen papae esset notorium de quo scandalizaretur ecclesia et ipse esset incorrigibilis," *C. Bened.*, p. 290. "Immo etiam si papa in hiis in quibus subest ecclesiae correctioni, ut in causa haeresis et in criminibus, in quibus incorrigibilis videtur. . . ," *Opus, Opera politica*, II, 794.

[84]Whatever the theoretical explanation might be, they could not conceive that the pope would have the power to hurt the "general welfare" of the Church, Tierney, *Conciliar Theory*, pp. 58-59, 66. Even Huguccio was able to rationalize only the case of heresy, pp. 61-63.

[85]Ibid., pp. 142, 228.

[86]"Quandocunque crimen eius est notorium . . . dicendum est ecclesiae . . . id est congregationi Romanorum. . . . Si autem Romani noluerint vel nequiverunt . . . ipsum iudicare, potestas iudicandi devolvitur ad quemcunque catholicum qui tanta praeditus potestate," *Octo*, Q. I, p. 63; ". . . iudicium primo spectet ad aliquas certas personas de clero; quibus deficientibus . . . hoc ad supremum principantem pertineat. . . . Ipso autem deficiente . . . ad quoscunque fideles qui tantam super ipsum temporalem valeant habere potestatem," ibid., Q. III, p. 121.

[87]*Dial.* I, p. 494, ll. 21-23.1

[88]Ibid., ll. 23-28.

[89]". . . ecclesiam constitutam in radice apostolicae sedis per successores episcoporum, hoc est ecclesiam tenentem doctrinam apostolicam, quam rexerunt successores episcopi (quamvis aliquando tale regimen fuerit interruptum). . . ," ibid., ll. 25-27.1

[90]See *An Argument in Defense of All Articles.* . . , trans. by C. M. Jacobs, *Works of Martin Luther*, Vol. III (Philadelphia: Holman Co., 1930), p. 87. *The Babylonian Captivity of the Church, Werke; kritische Gesammtausgabe*, ed. by J. K. F. Knaake, et. al. VI (Weimar: H. Böhlau, 1888), 565-67. *De votis monasticis Martini Lutheri iudicium, Werke; kritische Gesammtausgabe*, VIII (1889), 597.

[91]". . . ab antiquo electiones praelatorum concessae fuerunt clericis, quia licet omnes clerici & laici habuerunt ius eligendi: de consensu tamen laicorum propter hoc quod clerici erant sapientiores et sanctiores laicis. . . ," *Dial.* III, Tr. II, p. 937, ll. 30-32.

[92]". . . quia illa quae spectant ad bonum commune & non competunt aliquibus ratione ordinis aut officii . . . per sapientiores & meliores & per quos potest bonum commune melius prosperari sunt tractanda," ibid., ll. 34-37.

[93]Ibid.

[94]"Et tamen in potestate extitit laicorum generalibus conciliis interesse. Sed si vices tacite vel expresse clericis commiserunt, arctari minime debuerunt. . . . Clerici eos excludere de iure non possunt." *Dial.* I, p. 605, ll. 2-5.

[95]"Quod omnes tangit, ab omnibus tractari & approbari debet, ut notatur in Gloss. *di. 96 c. ubinam.* . . Sed ea quae tractantur in concilio generali omnes tangunt: quia in concilio generali tractari debet de fide & de aliis quae ad omnes pertineant Christianos. Igitur laici quos tangunt generalia concilia licite si voluerint poterunt interesse," ibid., p. 604, ll. 26-30.

[96]"Ubicunque ecclesiastica potestas deficit, laici habent iurisdictionem intra ecclesiam, hoc est, super clericos," ibid., p. 622, ll. 27-28. Also *Dial.* III, Tr. II, pp. 929-30.

[97]"Principes et laici in casibus pluribus habent potestatem super clericos et super papam

haereticum absque constitutione ecclesiae, et non solum per constitutionem ecclesiae, sed ex iure divino talem obtinent potestatem in casu," *C. Bened.*, p. 314.

[98]*Dial.* III, Tr. I, p. 815, ll. 17-23.

[99]Ibid., ll. 18-21. It is evident from this consideration alone—and more will be taken up below in ch. ii—how seriously mistaken Köhler, pp. 51-52, is in regarding Scripture as Ockham's sole ultimate norm of the Church's Faith and life.

[100]"Non totaliter ecclesiam suam optimo generi obligavit [Christus]: quin in casu manifestae necessitatis vel utilitatis posset illum modum regendi omittere vel mutare, nullum scilicet eligendo, vel eligendo plures, si id communitati fidelium manifeste expediret, vel aliquod illorum facere cogeretur," ibid., p. 866, ll. 57-59.

[101]See Gordon Leff's perceptive discussion of Ockham's conception of radical contingency, *William of Ockham*, pp. 616, 624. McGrade, *Political Thought*, p. 226, calls "hierocratic" those thinkers who "tended to treat as part of the unchangeable nature of things institutions to which Ockham gave a contingent, functional status." But this is precisely to miss his radicalism. Who else at that time would grant that Christ had instituted this structure and yet imply that his wishes were merely contingent? McGrade implies that any other view of the papal office proceeds from "abstract metaphysics" (p. 91) or has a "philosophical," "metaphysical" basis (p. 198, n. 2). But formal ecclesiology, that late blooming flower on the theological plant, was unanimous in giving that office a purely positive legal basis, as does Ockham himself. But that basis, the divine enactment, appeared unassailable.

[102]*Dial.* III, Tr. I, 1. 60.

[103]"Quamvis Christus ordinaverit, quod omnes fideles debeant uni summo pontifici obedire: quia tamen ista ordinatio Christi fuit affirmativa, & non negativa, bene obligat ad semper, sed non pro semper, & sic non est necesse quod omnes fideles omni tempore uni papae obediant . . . & quamvis omnes fideles debeant esse semper parati pro loco & tempore & modo debito, summo pontifici obedire: electio tamen summi pontifici . . . potest deferri . . . ad centum annos vel ducentum vel plures," ibid., Tr. II, p. 878, ll. 54-62, *passim.*

2 OCKHAM'S CUMULATIVE-DISTRIBUTIVE TREATMENT OF THE CHURCH

As we observe Ockham pursue the disengagement of the essential reality of the Church from its structures, the bifurcation in his view of the Church becomes more and more apparent. He sees its hierarchically structured institution as originating in Christ's action and possessing divine authorization; but at the same time he sees its inmost reality—the union of true believers—as having a divine guarantee which at any time might dissociate it from the divinely authorized structure. It is not particularly surprising that Ockham should have felt it necessary to attempt his disengagements or to adopt this bifurcated view. He could not see the teaching of John XXII as orthodox, let alone infallible; and papal conduct towards the partisans of Michael of Cesena and the adherents of Lewis of Bavaria made it virtually impossible for him to believe that in these matters the pope was really acting with the authority of Christ. Could it even be said that he was acting with the authority of the Church?

Let us try to see Ockham's problem somewhat as he may have seen it. If the reality of the Church could not be detached from the conduct of the papal office, then, since that office by structural necessity acted for the whole Church, whatever the pope did officially would commit the reality of the Church as such. But Christ had prayed that the faith of the Church might never fail at any time, and promised that he would be with the Church all times. If the pope could teach the Church heresy and behave in a way which gravely jeopardized the common good of believing, then the prayer of Christ had been in vain, his promise invalidated. Ockham apparently had found himself forced by considerations such as these, if by no others,[1] to the conclusion that the prayer and promise were given to the Church not as hierarchical structure, but as the totality of believers. In terms of the prayer and promise of Christ, then, the Church must be treated not as a structure but as the unstructured multitude of believers. In such a multitude even the highest office is only a part and cannot speak for the whole. The whole, in this view of things, is not other than the sum of the parts.[2]

Thus, a different treatment of the Church as a whole occurs in Ockham along with the treatment of its structures and markedly in preference to it. This treatment takes no account of the Church's structure but concerns itself only with the Church as an aggregate of all members:

> The Church, which is the multitude of all Catholics . . .[3]

> For these things are called "churchly" from the church, not that which is the pope or the congregation of clerics, but that which is the congregation of the faithful, which includes clergy and laity, men and women.[4]

> The Church, or the congregation of the faithful . . . is many true and real persons.[5]

It is significant that this treatment of the Church as aggregate occurs precisely where one would have expected the structured, hierarchical view, i.e., in the interpretation of those texts which were *loci classici* for justifying the claims of the institutional Church of the Middle Ages (e.g. Matt 28:20; Lk 22:31; Matt 16:19). Ockham was doing nothing unusual in explaining the words of promise to the apostles ("I am with you all days. . . ," Matt 28:30) and more especially of prayer for Peter's faith ("I have prayed for you that your faith fail not. . . ," Lk 22:31-21) as addressed to the entire Church of every age. What is unusual is Ockham's stress that the Church which is so addressed is the Church considered as the sum of its parts:

> That which applies to the whole Church must not be attributed to part of the Church, even the principal part.[6]

> That which is promised to the whole and to no part, ought not to be attributed to any part, even the more important. But . . . this promise was made to no part.[7]

Again and again he insists that no part, however important in terms of structure, is the object of this promise:

> But all the Masters in theology and even all the others in a general council apart from the pope are not that whole Church for which Christ petitioned.[8]

His point in each case is that no one part of the Church (pope, bishops, theologians, or a general council apart from the pope) can be the adequate object of the prayer and the promise of Christ, since the latter are for the whole Church. Thus in what is *most important* to the Church (the prayer and promise of Christ), no part, however eminent, can function for the whole. Ockham is here ignoring the necessary implications of structure as such—an unusual procedure indeed. His treatment deliberately sets aside a structured-hierarchical whole, in favor of an unstructured whole, the sum of all believers. It will be characteristic of him to speak of the Church as fellowship in terms which accentuate its plurality over its hierarchical unity.

So preoccupied is he with the Church as plurality of persons that he changes the traditional emphasis on the universality of belief[9] to an emphasis on the plurality of persons who have held that belief across the ages. Thus, he speaks of the believing members of the Church as cumulatively a motive for faith:

> The Church, which is the multitude of all Catholics who have been since the times of the prophets and apostles . . .[10]

> For that Church, which included the Apostles and Evangelists and martyrs and doctors, and all Catholics, up to the time of Augustine . . .[11]

> For this Church . . . also includes all the Catholic peoples up to the present.[12]

His language makes it clear that Ockham is considering more than a mere aggregate, a collective reality whose authority is simply its consensus. It appears that for him what counts is not just the collection, but the *accumulation* of members. The collectivity *grows* and accumulates ever more authority. The merely collective, like the cumulative, abstracts from the consideration of structure: but, unlike the cumulative conception, the collective whole *assembles* without intensifying. Its value is its unity. Ockham's appeal to tradition in the form of an accumulation of believing persons shows that the value of tradition for him is not only its *unity*, but also its *intensity*, i.e., the ever-growing strength and authority of its consensus. The relationship (and superiority) of whole to part is drawn not on a static but on an enlarging scale, and this growth is the special mark of Ockham's interest in tradition and of his conception of the historic whole of the Church.

He sees the Church of the present as having accumulated; and he sees the Church instituted and addressed by Christ as a reality which *will* accumulate, so that his words will be fully valid only for the whole that has accumulated throughout history. In this sense the Church lacking any of its parts and in any *single* historical period is less than the whole, less than the full object of Christ's grant and promise:

> For this Church, which includes the Apostles, Evangelists, all the Roman pontiffs and the other bishops and prelates . . . and all the Catholic peoples up till these times, seems to be of greater authority than . . . the Church which stands now in this pilgrimage.[13]

Though, as will be shown, Ockham regards the universal Church of any time as infallible, the whole community accumulated from the past is, so to speak, "more" infallible:

> The people should believe the whole community of preceding faithful more than the multitude existing in the present life . . .[14]

Clearly his polemical object is to relativize the authority of the present Church, in thrall to Avignon, by appealing to its past. It is more as an untended implication than as a conscious position that he leaves us to conclude that somehow the Church of any one time does not have full possession of her destined being, that the completed reality of the Church awaits the (accumulated) "fullness of times."

The Church as "Mystical Body"

While it is true that Ockham's treatment of the Church-whole as an accumulation rather than as a hierarchical institution or mere collectivity is so pronounced as to constitute a trademark, account must nonetheless be taken of those instances in which he acknowledges a different facet of the tradition and speaks of the Church as not only a structured but even an organic reality—where, that is, he uses the traditional "organismic" expression, "corpus misticum." [sic]

It should be remembered that the Ockham of the Church-political writings is a polemicist. Any acceptable argument against an adversary or supportive of his position might be expected to be pressed into service, especially if the argument in question were one utilized by an opponent. (He spends a large part of the fourth question of the *Octo quaestiones* quoting Lupold of Bebenberg against himself.)[15] It has been shown by Gierke and others[16] that the traditional doctrine of the *corpus mysticum* had been presed into service by the papal publicists to authorize the temporal supremacy of the papacy. There is an initial likelihood then that Ockham will try to use the doctrine against them, and so he does.

We saw above[17] that Ockham was engaged in the *Contra Benedictum* in defending the unity and juridical identity of the Church—and by application the Franciscan order—against the charge of John XXII that such a group is only a fictitious, imaginary person.[18] In this context he refers to the "mystical body":

> Just as the Church or the congregation of the faithful, although it is not one unique person, is many real and true persons because it is the mystical body of Christ which is true persons. . . . [He then quotes 1 Cor 12 on the unity of the body, one in many members.]From which . . . it is surely apparent that all the faithful are one body, one congregation, and one Church.[19]

This text is typical of the way in which he tends to use the doctrine, i.e., mostly when he is concerned to counter a curial or papal position based in some way upon the term.[20] All of this is not to say that in using this mode of expression Ockham is only engaging in argument *ad hominem* or *redargutio*, but it does suggest that the use of an expression is not of itself an adequate indication of the author's own genuine conviction, especially when it appears in largely polemical contexts.

Another consideration is perhaps more decisive. It concerns the shift in meaning and the serious alteration in connotation which occurred in the course of the thirteenth century in the use of the doctrine of the "mystical body." De Lubac has shown[21] that the term *corpus mysticum*, as used in the ninth century, referred to the Eucharist, as the sign *in mysterio* which effected the "true" body of Christ, the Church. No ancient or medieval writer had used the term *corpus mysticum* of the Church until the thirteenth century.[22] As a result of the Eucharistic controversies the word "true" had supplanted the word "mystical" to designate the sacramental body. Then the word "mystical" came to supplant the word "true" to designate the ecclesial body, though at first to call the Church the "mystical Body" amounted to a contraction for "body mystically signified by the sacrament."[23]

At the same time another use of "unity" was developing beside that designating the relationship between Christ's sacramental and ecclesial bodies. The unity of the ecclesial body was coming to be conceived as many members really being one.[24] Not the unity between the Church and the glorified body of Christ (or the sacramental body in the Eucharist), but the unity of all the members with each other as well as with Christ came to the fore. This unity was conceived after the analogy both of the human body and of human society, according to the famous precedent Aristotle had set in his *Politics*.[25] The emphasis on the union of faith and grace receded in favor of what was clearly an analogy for a social union. De Lubac observes that during the thirteenth century the old formulas like "mystical" all too often became little more than empty terms.[26] The "corpus ecclesiae" could be conceived— and more and more was conceived—as nothing more than a vast ensemble, called a body by a banal metaphor.[27] In this fashion it came to be used by those around the pope to claim supreme power for him, a power not at all mystical in the sense of sacramental and spiritual, but very juridical and political indeed.[28] In such an application to the social order, especially to political power struggles, the designation "mystical body" suffered degeneration and lost its spiritual resonance.[29] The unity it imported was not unity in the heavenly body of Christ, nor unity by means of the sacramental body in the Eucharist, nor even the spiritual unity of the Church in faith and grace, but rather the social and cultural unity of Christendom.[30]

Against this background the relatively few and always incidental references which Ockham makes to the "corpus mysticum" have no particular significance for his ecclesiology. While he does reserve the term as a description for the Church,[31] there is nothing to suggest that his use of it is other than conventional. His interest in it, at any rate, was not sufficient to distract him from the habitual pursuit of the cumulative view of the Church-whole.

The distributive treatment of the cumulative whole

There would seem to be no internal reason why this cumulative conception of the Church-whole, viewing its growth through the ages, should stop short of saying that only the fully-accumulated whole is the true object of the prayer and the promise of Christ, and indeed it has been shown that Ockham sees the Church of any one age as less in authority than the Church since the Apostles. The whole which the latter is must be at least in some way greater than the part which is the former. Ockham, however, does not treat the Church of any one age as a part only. It is truly the Church. We might say that it is the adequate, but not exhaustive object of the prayer and the promise of Christ.[32] Somewhere in the Church of any age, i.e., the Church of the living, the true Faith indefectibly survives.[33] It survives because Christ prayed that our faith "fail not," and promised that he would be with us "all days" till the end. To "fail not" means for Ockham "never to fail," the "never" being interpreted *semper et pro semper*, applying to every moment of time. The "all days" is interpreted with strict logic to mean "each and every day."[34] Thus the prayer and promise of Christ entail a *distribution* of the eschatological Church-whole in time, place, and members which prevents Ockham from treating the Church-whole always as the sum of its parts. A conception of whole in which prayer and promise are realized only in the complete accumulation of its parts at the end of time would deny the Church any meaningful historical existence. There must be a distributive application of prayer and promise in each age of the Church, so that the Church can function effectively in every age. This is the reason why Ockham must consider the Church of each age as the adequate object of prayer and promise. But this distributive treatment of the application of prayer and promise is, as such, and apparently apart from Ockham's conscious intention, a distributive consideration of the Church-whole. And the distribution does not stop at that level. By a curious turnabout in reasoning Ockham moves from the position that the guarantees of Christ *must* operate in each age to the contrasting idea that they cannot operate in all members in any age. Herewith he shifts to a distributive view of the Church's guarantees. Who could conceive that the prayer and promise of Christ would be validated in each and every member of the Church, and only in this way be verified of the cumulative whole of each age? Such a conception would involve denying that there had ever been even one heretic or apostate. The concrete fact of heresy (and one might well believe that the pronouncements of John XXII lurk in the background here) is thus decisive for a different principle in Ockham's treatment of the Church. Above[35] it was shown that Ockham saved the infallibility of the Church by maintaining that what was promised to the whole cannot apply to the part, the whole being greater than the part. Now he is in the position of maintaining that what was said of the whole *must* apply to a part—not to each part, of course, nor to any *determinate* part, but at least to *some* part. The cumulative whole has now been distributed—or more precisely, is now being considered distributively, in terms not of the accumulation but of the "return" of the function of the whole to the parts.[36]

A striking instance of this distributive treatment of the Church-whole occurs relatively early in the course of his polemical writings, in the *Contra Joannem*. It is a description of the process whereby the Church approves something, without judicial sentence, as Catholic truth:

> When prelates and people in common . . . confess the same truths expressed in plain words as expressly or tacitly Catholic. . . . But this happens whenever some Catholic truths are publicly asserted and preached through all Catholic regions, and published as Catholic among all Catholic peoples and no Catholic is found who resists such an assertion.[37] (Italics mine)

It is not merely a question of making sure that all the "parts" are accounted for, so that the whole will be really a whole. (Total unanimity, as has been pointed out, is not easy to envision.) The point of the inventory is that any dissenting voice might represent the true object of Christ's prayer and promise and might thus be witness to the true Faith.[38] Any difference of opinion immediately invokes the distributive treatment of the whole. Ockham sees this distribution in terms of larger groups and bodies within the Church,[39] but he is quite serious in taking it in terms of individual believers:

> If only one should dissent, such a truth must not be accepted.[40]

This is the context for perhaps his most famous ecclesiological statement:

> The whole faith of the Church can stand in one alone.[41]

This text is particularly noteworthy not primarily because in lapidary fashion it states that the individual believer is also the object of Christ's prayer and promise, but because it declares that in some way, the whole as object of prayer and promise can be present *with* a single believer. Unusual as this position may be, it is hardly an exotic intrusion into an otherwise traditional ecclesiological enterprise. Rather it appears to be the inevitable outcome of a confrontation between Ockham's view of social wholes and his adherence both to the words of Christ and the infallibility of the Church.

In Ockham's view, the reality of order is not something other than or apart from the ordered parts themselves:

> The order or unity [of the universe] is not something in reality distinct from all the parts of the universe.[42]

The whole for Ockham has no reality of its own apart from the being-ordered of the parts. Order itself—and thus wholeness—is to be accepted as contingent fact: it cannot be shown to be essential or necessary. Since existence, pertains only to irreducibly single things, real relationships are always historical matters of fact, not necessary in themselves or absolute, but only contingent. For Ockham the ordering of the Church-whole was the salvific work of Christ. The entire being of the Church is something which stems solely from the merciful will of God, and upon God's will neither essence nor necessity can make any claim.[43] The order of the Church, which exists only by the divine, instituting will, is not other than the being-ordered of the members of the Church; and yet, strangely, the Church as object of prayer and promise can be something other than, indeed less than, the sum of all its parts.

As was said above,[44] Christ's words of prayer and promise cannot apply for Ockham to the Church as structured. The structured view of the Church sees the papal office acting by structural necessity for the whole Church, so that the pope acting officially would commit the reality of the Church as such. But the Avignon papacy was guilty of heresy. For the Church to be committed to that heresy would invalidate prayer and promise. On the other hand, although Ockham never explicitly deals with this consideration, prayer and promise cannot apply to the Church as the *sum* of all its members, since even the error (not to mention heresy) of one member would invalidate prayer and promise *as applying* to that sum-total. Thus, if prayer and promise must always be efficacious, they must be able to be verified of something less than all the members—of some of the members, or, by logical extension, of even one member.

This conclusion does not at all mean that the Church in that case would have shrunk to one member. It is true that the formal heretic is *ipso facto* cut off from the Church, but, as Ockham sees the prayer and promise, the belief of the Church (*fides qua creditur*) is a belief in an objective Faith (*fides quae creditur*), the perpetuation of which is the specific object of Christ. Viewed objectively, the true Faith departs not only from formal heretics but from all those who innocently believe error or heresy. The latter are still in and of the Church but are no longer the realized object of prayer and promise. There is a real difference then in the number of those who are members of the Church and of those who believe the true Faith. This difference keeps Ockham's reasoning from being the circular procedure Lagarde accuses him of indulging in: the totality of the Church is never infected with heresy, but the Church is the assembly of those not so infected.[45] The latter part of that statement is incorrect (or else uses "Church" in an equivocal sense).

Ockham, constrained by his belief in the efficacy of Christ's words of promise, has thus arrived at a position his philosophy would not of itself have afforded. The Church-whole which is the object of the prayer and promise of Christ is other than and less than the sum of its parts, and it is a reality detachable from any of them in particular. That is, it is a distributive reality. The part has become (as object of prayer and promise) that which bears the reality of the whole. A cumulative treatment of the whole must, so as to take account of the prayer and promise of Christ, be accompanied by a distributive one as well, the price of departing from structural views of what Christ intended. But this distributive treatment must not be dismissed as no more than Ockham's way of viewing the Church-whole. The faith is actually distributed among the members at all times. And when, by the error or defection of some (or most) it remains in only a few (or even in one), a new pattern of distribution actually appears. There is a real, new "subsistence" of the whole in the part. It would be even a greater mistake to think of this "distributive view" of Ockham's as a purely formal (and artificial) way for the observer to characterize certain of his ecclesiological statements. Ockham's Church really functions for him in the way this term describes. The process, strange though it sounds, can be characterized.

Devolvement

To begin with, Ockham makes it clear that a distributive treatment of prayer and promise could not follow a structural course. The reality of the Church's faith and life must be present somewhere at all times; but, given human freedom, unpredictability, and the *status viatorum*,[46] official prerogatives and responsibilities cannot determine where that reality will be and how it will operate. The problem is not the office but the faith of the office-holder. The distribution of the Church's faith must be able to be altered, its pattern changed, its location shifted. There must be a process, apart from structured procedure, wherein those in the truth fall into error or heresy, while those in error or heresy recover the truth. What is required in principle is an inner dynamic, a possibility of shift and transfer which can be called "devolvement,"[47] that is, an inner transfer of the efficacious reality of the Church from the aggregate whole down to some part, or, in the case of the hierarchical whole, from the higher office to the lower, the clergy to the laity, the larger to the smaller group, etc. As Ockham uses "devolvement" it is rather more precise to say, not that the *locus* of the Church's faith shifts (though it does), but that, in consequence of the fact that now one group (or person), now another, is left in possession of the true Faith, the capacity and responsibility for valid and efficacious action in the life of the Church shifts from one to the other:

> Anyone in the Church militant is left in the hand of his own counsel, that he might remain in the Faith according to his own free decision . . . or that he might deviate from Catholic belief. But the community of Christians is so preserved by God that if one were to wander far from faith another will endure in faith by the gift of God; whence if the pope should err against faith, another Christian, man or woman, will not at all recede from faith.[48]

Ockham is daring enough to locate devolvement at the very foundation of the Church, in the heart of the apostolic college itself:

> Although any one of the apostles of himself could have deviated from the truth, as Peter actually did, nevertheless the college of apostles could not err. Wherefore, when Peter erred, in no way did the college of apostles err, but one of them, that is, Paul, corrected him.[49]

Each apostle could err, but the college (i.e., the whole) could not. Paul *is*, functionally, the whole and acts in that capacity.

The word "devolve" itself is used by Ockham precisely to characterize this transfer of responsibility and capacity for efficacious action:

> Just as (according to the promise of Christ) Catholic faith will remain till the end of the world, so will the power of coercing heretics by right . . . remain in the Church; but if the pope with all the clergy should be a heretic, *the legal power of coercing heretics* would not be in the pope and clergy. . . . Therefore, in that case *the power of coercing heretics would by right devolve to the laity.*[50]

It should be noticed first, that Ockham grounds devolvement in the possession of "Catholic faith," second, that the devolvement concerns a legal right, and third, that the legal right can devolve to the laity from the structure of Church offices. Thus Ockham is not working in the necessity-knows-no-law frame of reference of the later conciliarists, as the phrase "de iure" indicates. What happens in devolvement, though occasioned by necessity in an emergency situation, will not be outside the law of the Church's operation.

Legally speaking, devolvement in these situations corresponds to official function for the whole. *But devolvement of function happens only because there has been a devolvement of faith*, an inner transfer of true believing or a concentration of it in fewer *loci*. Thus devolvement involves what official function of itself never can: the presence of the whole with the part. The pope himself could be, as an individual believer, the term of such a devolvement of faith, but only as believer, not as pope, would he speak or act *with the presence of the whole*. The whole faith of the Church, the Church as object of prayer and promise, is present in those to whom it has devolved.

Devolving dissociation from external Church

The cumulative view of the Church-whole abstracts from any consideration of structure without denying it. But in the distributive view, when devolvement takes place, there is a real dissociation from the external reality of the Church which assaults the Church's structure. His contempt for the institutional Church of his day he barely attempts to conceal. The famous statement that the whole faith of the Church can stand in one member[51] occurs in many places and many forms in his *Dialogus*,[52] in some of which he makes explicit his judgment that the intentions of Christ do not need the institutional Church and are adequately fulfilled even in a few or in only one:

> The eternal law of salvation would not have been given in vain by Christ even though the greater part of the faithful, even all except a very few, or except one should err . . .[53] For the same promise of Christ would stand if . . . all should be infected except two or three.[54]

And most explicitly of all:

> In one alone [the whole faith] could endure, because on account of one alone whatever Christ promised the Apostles could be preserved . . .[55]

Such statements had not always been made from animus towards the Church. In one sense his position is only a systematic extension of an idea taken from the Marian devotional literature of the previous centuries: that during the Passion of Christ the faith of the Church endured in Mary alone.[56] His contribution, here as elsewhere, is to find in an exceptional situation a principle of function.[57]

Mention should also be made of the fact that, at least twice, Ockham adds an indefectibility and therefore a devolvement of grace to that of faith, although, based as it is on the promise of Christ given to faith, the former he seems to see as a consequence of the latter:

Disciple: What if no one should be solicitous as he ought to be?
Teacher: The answer is that, just as the faith will never fail until the end of the world, so there will always be someone in grace, and solicitous in the proper way about those things which are necessary for the Church of God. But if no one should be solicitous . . . all would be outside of grace and in mortal sin, something which will never happen.[58]

Although the universal Church . . . be not able so to err against the faith or be so stained by mortal sin that no one would be in true faith and charity . . .[59]

In all of these reflections upon possibilities of devolvement one is able to see most clearly just how far Ockham is willing to go in his distributive treatment of the Church. If the cumulative view abstracts from structure, this distributive view is ready to dissociate the Church as object of prayer and promise not only from the Church's structure but from almost all of the members as well.

Relationship of cumulative and distributive views

We have seen that the cumulative treatment of the Church-whole occasioned a distributive treatment, in order to take adequate account of the historic fulfillment of Christ's prayer and promise. If there is both a cumulative and a distributive functioning of the whole, did Ockham conceive them as alternating, mutually exclusive functions, or rather in some more directly related way? Precisely what is the reality of the cumulative aspect when the Church functions distributively, and what is the reality of the distributive when the Church functions as a cumulative whole?

Since he never manifested any consciousness of using either view systematically, it is not surprising that he never attempted a systematic explanation of the relationship of the two views. There is a passage where he illustrates a question about Church office with logical principles which govern the collective or distributive consideration of a plurality. This brief passage is the only place where the two attitudes might be said to be joined, but even here he does not explicitly apply the principles to the Church-whole.[60] It appears that he moved from the distributive view to the cumulative and back again as the circumstances and requirements of the argument of the moment dictated without ever troubling himself about the ultimate unity or coherence of his position.

There are elements in his thinking, however, which make it possible to bring cumulative and distributive views together in something like a relationship of reciprocal dependence. As directed to the day-to-day life of the Church's members, the prayer and promise of Christ always function distributively and disjunctively in the Church, that is, in one part or another. Ockham says that in the Church one can have doctrinal certitude even though each individual taken separately can err and has no special protection, because the community will be preserved from error so that if one deviates from the faith the other will not.[61] Thus there is, in theory at least, a constant actual devolution of faith as we have seen.

What then of the cumulative view of the Church? Does the Church ever function as a cumulative whole insofar as its faith is the object of Christ's prayer and promise? The answer to that question must acknowledge those numerous passages in which Ockham speaks of the Church of all ages since the apostles as truly being the Church in the full sense of the word, the strictly universal Church.[62] This universal Church is not meant to be merely mental, an addition of the mind. The Church through the ages has obviously for Ockham a real unity, a total being, an effective function.[63] But we have already seen what that function is: the function of absolute, irrefragable norm of Faith. It is what is more commonly referred to as tradition, translated, as was said, into the plurality of the Church's members throughout history and the cumulative weight of their individual faiths. The total, cumulative Church of the past exists in the present as tradition.[64]

However there is something more to be said about the cumulative function. Earlier it was pointed out that Ockham sees the Church as having accumulated, and, as Christ founded it, a reality which *would* accumulate.[65] *As such* it received the prayer and promise of Christ. This means that the Church of any age —and any local Church or group or individual—can be the object of prayer and promise only through the cumulative whole, only as a part of that whole. Thus the distributive function depends upon the reality of the accumulated whole in the intention of God and as real object of His act in Christ. Especially is it true that any further "redistribution" or relocation of the Faith-whole, i.e., devolvement, cannot take place unless somehow the accumulated whole *is*, at least in the divine intention.

It thus appears that the summary answer to our question is that the reality of the cumulative function of the Church, when the Church is functioning distributively, is as *ground*, in the divine intention, of the distribution, and as *tradition* in the historical record of the Church's faith. This means that the universal Church of all believers in all ages, because it alone is the ultimate object of Christ's prayer and promise, is the object of the abiding divine power which preserves, and, when necessary, transfers the inner efficacious reality of the Church's life. The universal Church of any one time, since it is an adequate and real object of prayer and promise, abides as the immediate ground, in the divine intention, of the regular distributive function and of whatever devolvement takes place. The totality of believers, without regard to the Church's structure, is seen by Ockham as effectively whole, for the sake of which the Faith of Christ is preserved and the divine power exerted.

In dependence upon this ideal cumulative wholeness of the Church the distributive function, as we have seen, is always actual. In the first place it is actual because the Faith which the whole Church believes *every* believer must adhere to *in toto*, and because the faith *by which* the whole Church believes is only the addition or reduplication of the faith of *each* believing member. The whole-function of believing is always distributed to (i.e. distributively present in) each true believer. But, in the second place, because there are always some who, knowingly or not, deviate from the Faith or fall into error, a further redistribution of faith is also always taking place. As the (objectively) true Faith departs from such members the pattern of its distribution changes and its location may even shift (devolve) to new, or newly orthodox, believers. The Church's inner life of faith (and grace), whether it abides with the pope, or a general council, or the universal episcopate, or the clergy, or only with the poor and unlettered, is in constant actual devolvement among the members of the Church, without regard to office, structure, or status. But the Faith which is preserved in devolvement of belief is the Faith of the cumulative whole of the Church, for the sake of which the devolvement of faith—and if need be, that devolvement of function—takes place. The cumulative whole is seen really to underlie that devolvement.

Revelation and the cumulative-distributive view

Ockham's cumulative and distributive treatments of the Church constitute for him characteristic and pervasive ecclesiological styles. Reflections of them or their consequences can be found in a broad range of ecclesiological themes. Perhaps one of the most interesting of their applications is to be seen in his doctrine of revelation, a doctrine which is still a vexed problem in Ockham research. In the past, as was noted earlier,[66] Ockham was considered a forerunner of the *sola scriptura* principle of the Reformation. Even now, as Oberman says, the research concerning his doctrine of Scripture has produced contradictory results. "Occamistic respect for the authority of Holy Scripture has been stressed at times to the point where it is identified with the *sola scriptura* principle of the Reformation," and on the other side stress has been laid on his "eclesiastical positivism" and submission to authoritative norms.[67] The fact is that Ockham's treatment of Scripture must be seen in the context of his over-all conception of revelation, which is not generally well understood.

The intention here is to consider this general conception of revelation, but from the restricted view of how it relates to his cumulative-distributive view of the Church. For this purpose a summary presentation of his discussion of the sources of revelation (i.e., where Catholic truths are to be found) will be sufficient, in order to show that what is distinctive about his view of revelation is related to his cumulative-distributive view of the Church. The attempt will be made to show that without taking account of this view one cannot adequately understand his doctrine of revelation.

Ockham never speaks of the "sources of revelation" (a later term), but rather of "Catholic truths"—where they are to be found, how they are given to the Church. His discussions speak conventionally of Sacred Scripture; but "tradition" is a rare word, used only in strict association with the Apostles, in the phrase "tradition of the Apostles."[68] The word never appears independently, as a technical term descriptive of a source or aspect of revelation.

"Revelation" for Ockham is a term with no very restricted meaning, as we shall see from the examination of two important passages. Christian revelation appears to refer to any truth which has come from God to the Church, whether through Christ, the Apostles, or someone else. For him revelatory possibilities are not confined to Apostolic or New Testament times.

In the First Part of the *Dialogus* Ockham gives us two extended statements of where the truths of revelation are to be found and of what other truths are necessarily implicated in belief. The statements are in substantial agreement. In the first of them, after recounting the opinion of those who say that only what is contained in Scripture or can be deduced from it by necessary consequence are Catholic truths and must be believed for salvation[69]—an opinion he appears definitely to reject—he tells us that there are many truths, belief in which is necessary for salvation, which are not explicitly in Scripture and cannot be inferred only from the contents of Scripture.[70] There are three kinds of these, he says:

> For certain [truths] are from God and from Christ according to his humanity, on which our salvation principally depends. . . . Others are truths on which our salvation does not thus principally depend: nonetheless it behooves us to hold them with firm faith, because . . . they have come from the revelation or approbation of God. . . . Some truths of this sort are contained outside the aforesaid canon [of Scripture] which nevertheless have come to Catholics through revelation and divine approbation by means of the Apostles, since Christ while he lived in mortal flesh with the apostles taught them many things . . . which are not in the Bible. . . . All these truths, and those things which can by necessary consequence be deduced from them . . . must be held by Catholics. . . . Besides, there are certain truths which cannot be concluded just from the contents of divine Scripture and the truths which have come to us through the Apostles but which follow from the aforesaid truths or from some one of them and certain other truths of fact which really cannot be denied. . . . Also . . . the deeds of the Church and of the saints.[71]

One scarcely knows how to limit the application of such inclusive principles. But the range, broad as it is, is enlarged in the second passage:

> . . . in Sacred Scripture, or the traditions of the Apostles, or historical chronicles, or revelations indubitably given to the faithful, or those things which follow from the foregoing or from one of them, or in a revelation or inspiration manifestly given in a divine manner.[72]

He organizes this multiplicity into five categories: a) Scripture, and its necessary consequences; b) extra-Scriptural Apostolic teaching coming to us orally or through the writings of believers; c) chronicles and histories written by believers; d) deductions from either a) or b) or from a) or b) by way of c); and e) new revelations or inspirations.[73] Of course, not all of these truths can be called "revelation" in the strict sense, as Ockham explicitly points out;[74] but revelation is implicated in them all, making them indisputable and obligatory as matters of belief:

> Whenever the Church rightly approves something, she bases herself in some one of the foregoing five classes of truths.[75]

He describes the truths deduced from revelation by way of certain others truths of fact, and also the deeds of the Church and of the saints, as revelation only in the broad sense of the term.[76] Actually he has not so much extended the categories of belief as he has merely explicitly accounted theological conclusions and dogmatic facts among those categories, a proceeding not very different from previous teaching.[77]

Various shorter versions of these categories appear:

> There is an opinion which holds that the divine Scriptures contained in the Bible and in the writers of the same sacred scripture, and in the universal Church and the Apostles must be believed in everything with no hesitation.[78]

Rather than detail each of these classes every time he must refer to the truths of Faith, he generally resorts to some short-hand or other:

> For if . . . they were to preach against the slightest assertion of the divine scripture or the universal doctrine they should in no way be believed but the rule of faith is to be firmly adhered to.[79]

"Universal doctrine" or "the doctrine of the universal Church" generally serves to summarize all the categories of Catholic truths outside of Scripture and the strict formal deductions therefrom.[80] The simplification is indeed warranted. We can agree with Oberman's perceptive and careful assessment that these five categories do in fact reduce themselves to two: scriptural and extra-scriptural revelation;[81] and it thereby becomes immediately clear that Ockham was not an early proponent of the Reformation principle of *sola scriptura*.[82]

The descriptions of Catholic truths recounted thus far have all been lists of what we would call the sources or "locations" of the Church's faith. They are descriptions of how the Church encounters and receives revelation. But occasionally there is another sort of statement of what must be believed. This other sort of statement concerns how the individual believer comes to know the faith of the Church and how this faith is promulgated. An example occurs in the *Contra Benedictum*, where Ockham tells us that the Catholic is bound to believe as divine Faith: 1) articles of Faith in the Creeds of the Church; 2) what he knows to be contained explicitly in the Scriptures; 3) things he knows to be defined by general councils or the Roman pontiffs in a Catholic way.[83] The typical and significant difference between the two sorts of statements is that the second includes what the first leaves out: the definitions of popes and councils. Such definitions for Ockham are practical means of promulgating and learning the Faith to the extent that they conform to "Catholic truths," the Church's belief. Of course it has never been traditional to consider ecclesiastical definitions as revelatory sources, but Ockham will not grant that they are of themselves inerrant formulations of revelation. They are not of themselves "Catholic truths." Popes and general councils are able to define only "in a Catholic way"—that is, *following the norms and observing the classes described.*[84] Their statements are sources neither of revelation nor of faith, but themselves must be governed by the sources. In the context of a discussion as to the status of the "determinations and definitions of the Church" (where he is therefore referring to the hierarchical Church), Ockham says:

> All the truths which the Church determines or defines are considered as included under some one of the five aforesaid kinds. . . . It is not in the power of the Church to approve or even to disapprove anything at will; but the Church has founded itself rightly when it approves whatever is in one of the five aforesaid classes of truths.[85]

In the same way Ockham says a truth can be called "Catholic" if, apart from other reasons, it has been approved by the pope. But then he makes it clear that the pope can approve such a truth only if it has been revealed to the Church in Scripture or in some other way:

> Then it must be asked whether the pope bases himself on some revelation or also sacred Scripture or the doctrine of the universal Church. Whichever it is, it follows that the supreme pontiff by his approbation does not establish that such a truth was and is Catholic.[86]

While a reception and belief by the universal Church marks a truth as Catholic, the *approval* (official) of either institutional Church or the pope does not make a truth Catholic:

> No truth is Catholic unless divinely revealed or inserted in the divine Scriptures, or known to the certitude of the universal Church, or deducible from one of them by necessary argument. But nothing of the foregoing is known to depend on the approbation of the supreme pontiff or even of the Church.[87]

To be sure, this is not to say that popes and councils may not or cannot define, nor that if they do, what they define need not be accepted (even in faith, if they define in a "Catholic way"). But the Faith-character of their definitions does not proceed from the revelatory or Faith-character of popes and councils as sources or even as teachers of Faith.[88] It proceeds from their having spoken in a Catholic way, instructed by the Faith. We have seen already that in terms of doctrinal reliability, doctors are to be preferred to prelates, even popes.[89]

The ultimate and irreducible sources of revelation for Ockham, then are two, but they are not Scripture and Tradition. They are rather to be characterized as Scriptural and non-Scriptural revelation, since non-Scriptural revelation is not to be equated with Tradition. It includes not only the non-Scriptural revelation given through the Apostles to successive generations of the Church, but, as we have seen, the possibility (if not the fact) of new revelations given to the Church. This category of new revelations is the place where a relationship to Ockham's cumulative-distributive view of the Church can be seen.

As Ockham describes it in the passages quoted above, this category of new, post-Apostolic, post-New Testament revelation has two characteristics. In the first place it has no determinate *locus* in the Church, much less an institutional or official *locus*. It apparently can happen anywhere and to anyone: it is unpredictable. While it would be overly schematic to see here a direct application of the distributive view of the Church or the devolving dynamic, there is clearly some relationship. This distributive view in any case makes it easy to envision a revelation springing up almost anywhere.

In the second place, the theoretical possibility of revelations at any time in the Church makes of revelation itself an *on-going* process. The Faith can receive an increment not only of understanding but also of divine disclosure. Earlier it was pointed out that what we would call "Tradition" Ockham speaks of as the cumulative witness of the believers of all ages, giving the Faith a constant increment of understanding and of certitude.[90] Now it can be added that there can be an increment of revelation itself. Revelation becomes in this way *cumulative*. The correspondence with his cumulative view of the Church is in this case even clearer. No claim is being made that Ockham's cumulative view of the Church produced of itself this cumulative view of revelation. Indeed his position here seems to be the product of his concern that God be understood as sovereignly free to do as He chooses:

> This is not impossible: because God could, if it pleased him, reveal or inspire Catholic truths anew.[91]

But the consequence of this freedom is that revelation has to be, in principle at least, cumulative. Again, that Ockham would have insisted upon this possibility becomes much more understandable in the light of his cumulative view of the Church.

The cumulative treatment of the Scriptures

Ockham's cumulative view of the Church illuminates another feature of his doctrine of revelation which at first sight is apt to seem puzzling if not paradoxical. This is the fact that in some perspectives he subordinates the Church to Scripture, while in others he subordinates Scripture to the Church.

While the Scriptures are not for Ockham the sole, they are indubitably the preeminent source of revelation. To this extent, those who have seen in him an early proponent of *sola scriptura* are not without all justification.[92] He can refer to Scripture as the "foundation of the whole Catholic faith," comprehending the "divine law," practically equivalent to what must be believed.[93] Nothing else taken by itself—neither the universal doctrine nor the Apostles—is ever called the "rule of faith," as Scripture is.[94] It is true, as in the last-quoted passage, that when he exalts Scripture alone, he is usually doing so not over against other revelatory sources but over against "popes and cardinals," "decrees and decretals."[95] He complains, for instance, that the Avignonese church tries to force theologians like himself into obedience "against reason and the sacred Scriptures."[96] There are, however, a few statements which cannot so easily be accounted for, not enough to bring his position into serious doubt, but enough to constitute a lapse of complete consistency.[97] At all events, it can be said that he gives stirring tribute to the importance and even preeminence of Scripture in the Church. Scripture, considered as a whole, is the foundation of the Church's faith; consequently the Church is subjected to it as to its rule of faith.

> The people should believe divine Scripture more than . . . all mortals . . .[98].

In view of this fact, it is interesting that what he says of Scripture as a whole he will not say of the individual evangelists. The author of a gospel does not enjoy as much authority for faith as does the universal Church of all ages, since he is only a part of its whole. In this perspective Ockham subordinates Scripture to the Church:

> The Church, which is the multitude of all Catholics who have been since the time of the prophets and apostles is more to be believed than a gospel: not because the gospel is in any way doubtful, but because the whole is greater than the part. Therefore the Church which is of greater authority than an evangelist is that Church of which the author of the gospel is designated a part.[99]

Even when he compares the authority of a gospel with that of the Church of the living alone, his description of its authority is tepid:

> This whole multitude of Christians now in the mortal life of the living is not of greater authority than is the holy gospel.[100]

By not clearly subjecting it to the gospel, he creates the suspicion that he might say that the authority of this multitude is also not *less* than that of a gospel. However that may be, he neither confirms nor allays the suspicion.

It is impossible to pursue this comparison of the relative authority of Scripture in its parts and the Church in its parts, not only because there are so few texts which can give us more than hints, but because this comparison was not Ockham's concern; indeed, he may not have realized that he was implying such evaluations. He was simply treating the Scriptures *as an accumulation which corresponded to the accumulation of the Church.*[101] The evangelist is not just part of the process of revelation: he is part of the Church. Does the whole of revelation, then, somehow correspond to the whole of the Church? Is the authority of the Church, then, really the same thing as the authority of revelation? He certainly appears to put the ultimate universal Church on a par with sacred Scripture:

. . . the concordant and unanimous approbation and confession of the universal Church . . . which is seen to be not less in authority . . . than even the authority of divine Scripture . . .[102]

In this view the Church itself tends to become the source of revelation in its accumulated whole. The faith of the universal Church is not only an infallible *norm* for revelation and the true Faith: it is the source itself, the whole of which the sacred writers, taken separately, are only a part. Somehow the Church is not *under* Scripture (taking the individual sacred writers separately), it comprehends the sacred writers.[103] The latter themselves are treated more as *believers*, giving witness to the Faith, than *revealers*, originating it. It is the accumulated wholeness of the Church, even in its organs of revelation, which adequately speaks for the Church's faith, not any determinate part or function, even the Scriptures.

Since Ockham never explicitly discussed the relationship between Scripture and Church as revelatory sources, conclusions here must be somewhat tentative. On two positions we can, however, have some degree of assurance: a) The Scriptures as a whole are (however inconsistently) an adequate (not exhaustive) expression, even the "foundation," of the Church's faith; and b) the individual sacred writings, i.e., a gospel, are less in authority of faith than is the universal Church of all ages. Scripture as a whole has an authority definitely greater than that of the individual parts. It is not difficult to conclude that Ockham's cumulative treatment of the Church has served at least as an inducement towards a cumulative view of the Scriptures as well, such is the pervasiveness of that cumulative view.

Conclusion

Ockham's cumulative-distributive treatment of the Church appears throughout as a strategy of considerable flexibility. In its cumulative aspect it permits him to subordinate the individual believer, whether pope or simple layman, to the authority of the whole and to set the Church of the past over against the Church of the present. At the same time, its distributive aspect allows him to claim for the individual believer, in particular circumstances, prerogatives which would ordinarily belong to the whole Church or its highest officers. The cumulative-distributive treatment makes room for the day-to-day function of the Church's official structure, while never unconditionally committing the inner reality of the Church to that structure. In the same way it leaves room for a truly representative function in the Church (the general council) while limiting the representation to matters of less than the highest importance, thereby protecting the freedom of the individual believer. The redistribution which takes place in devolvement of Faith and function provides a rationale for a wide variety of occasional and emergency interventions in or interruptions of official function, while neither challenging the basic validity of the regular function nor according equal status to the exceptional measure.

It may indeed be suspected that Ockham hit upon his cumulative-distributive treatment of the Church-whole in order to accomplish these adjustments, since it did undeniably prove a very adaptable ecclesiological device. The versatility and elusiveness of the standards he uses to bring the Avignonese church to judgment testify to its polemical adaptability as well. But it is above all an eloquent testimony to the sense of freedom he feels as he confronts the structures of the Church. In dealing with them he appears to feel that he is dealing with human contingencies only incidentally touched by divine imperatives. The transcendence of the faith has decisively attentuated the order of the Church.

[1]There is always the possibility that he proceeded, consciously or not, from certain 'nominalist' predilections in his ecclesiological and political thinking viz., that politics and institutional structures are not realities distinct from the component members. Such conclusions risk overlooking the fact that Ockham did not 'think away' social realities or the reality of relationships but only their inadmissible 'hypostatizations.'

[2]Leff, *William of Ockham*, p. 637, has not seen that the antinomy for Ockham was not between office and institution but between the *whole institutional structure* and the *believers.*

[3]"Ecclesia, quae est multitudo catholicorum omnium. . . ," *Dial.* I, p. 400, l. 50.

[4]"Vere enim denominantur 'ecclesiastica' ab ecclesia non quae est papa aut congregatio clericorum, sed ab ecclesia quae est congregatio fidelium quae clericos et laicos, viros et mulieres comprehendit," *Octo*, Q. I, p. 65.

[5]"Ecclesia sive congregatio fidelium . . . est plures verae personae et reales," *C. Bened.*, p. 191. The context here is of special interest. Ockham is defending the collective juridical identity of the Franciscan order and of the Church against the pope's charge that the order is an imaginary person. Even in defending its collective identity, Ockham is constrained to mention the Church's plurality.

[6]"Quod competit toti ecclesiae, non est attribuendum parti ecclesiae, etiam principali," *Dial.* I, p. 478, ll. 41-42.

[7]"Illud q[uod] promittitur toti & nulli parti, non debuit alicui parti attribui, etiam principaliori. Sed . . . nulli parti fuit hoc promissum," ibid., p. 489, ll. 33-35.

[8]"Sed omnes Magistri in Theologia & etiam omnes alii a Papa in generali concilio non sunt tota illa ecclesia pro qua Christus rogavit," ibid., p. 432, ll. 1-2.

[9]". . . quod ubique, quod semper, quod ab omnibus creditum est. . . ," Vincent of Lerins, *Commonitorium*, II, 3 (ed. by Reginald S. Moxon; Cambridge, England: Cambridge University Press, 1915), p. 10.

[10]"Ecclesia, quae est multitudo catholicorum omnium, qui fuerunt a temporibus prophetarum et apostolorum. . . ," *Dial.* I, p. 402, ll. 50-51.

[11]"Illa enim ecclesia, quae Apostolos et Evangelistas ac martyres et doctores, universosque catholicos, usque ad tempora Augustini comprehendit. . . ," *C. Joann.*, p. 66.

[12]"Haec enim ecclesia . . . omnesque catholicos populos usque ad haec tempora comprehendit," ibid.

[13]"Haec enim ecclesia, quae Apostolos, Evangelistas, omnes Romanos pontifices ceterosque

episcopos ac praelatos . . . omnesque catholicos populos usque ad haec tempora comprehendit, maioris auctoritatis esse videtur quam . . . ecclesia, quae nunc in hac peregrinatione consistit," ibid., p. 66.

[14]"Magis credet populus toti communitati fidelium praecedentium quam multitutini existentium pulus toti communitati fidelium praecedentium quam multitutini existentium in vita praesenti," *Dial.* I, p. 616, ll. 12-13.

[15]Pp. 126-57.

[16]Otto Gierke, *Political Theories of the Middle Age*, trans. F. W. Maitland (Boston: Beacon Press, 1958), p. 22. John A. Watt, *The Theory of Papal Monarchy in the Thirteenth Century* (London: Burns & Oates, 1965), pp. 104-5. Ernest Kantorowicz, *The King's Two Bodies: A Study in Medieval Political Theology* (Princeton: Princeton University Press, 1957), p. 194. Henri de Lubac, *Corpus mysticum: L'Eucharistie et L'Église au moyen âge* (Paris: Aubler, 1949), p. 100.

[17]Ch. ii, n. 17.

[18]*C. Bened.*, p. 190. See Maitland "Introduction," in Gierke, *Political Theories*, pp. xiv-xx, where Maitland discusses the "fiction theory," attributed by Gierke to Innocent IV, in which the fictitious person, such as a corporation, is capable of ownership but not of those things which are matters of fact (e.g., acting in some way).

[19]"Quemadmodum ecclesia sive congregatio fidelium, licet non sit unica persona, est plures verae personae et reales, quia est corpus Christi misticum, quod est verae personae. . . . Ex quibus . . . patet aperte quod omnes fideles sunt unum corpus, una congregatio, et una ecclesia.," *C. Bened.*, p. 190.

[20]E.g., *Dial.* I, p. 494, ll. 9-12. *Dial.* III, Tr. II, p. 930, ll. 32-38. *Octo*, Q. I, p. 60.

[21]*Corpus mysticum*, p. 18.

[22]Ibid.

[23]Ibid., pp. 104-7, 279, 281.

[24]Ibid., pp. 99-100.

[25]Ibid., p. 129.

[26]Ibid., p. 291.

[27]Ibid., p. 100.

[28]Gierke, *Political Theories*, p. 22.

[29]*Corpus mysticum*, pp. 129-30.

[30]Watt, *Papal Monarchy*, p. 104, observes that the meaning of *corpus mysticum* became "politicized." Kantorowicz, *The Kings Two Bodies*, p. 202, calls it a "relatively colourless sociological, organological, or juristic notion." It came to denote merely the Christian polity or Christendom, Watt, p. 105. Some publicists (e.g., John of Paris) spoke of two bodies: the "natural" body, which is all mankind, the "mystical" body, which is the Church, de Lubac, *Corpus mysticum*, p. 131.

[31]See *above*, p. 72.

[32]*Dial.* I, p. 497, ll. 53-58.

[33]"Ad ecclesiam etiam universalem si convenire posset, esset principaliter appelandum. Si vero Christianitas tantum esset pravitate infecta haeretica quod Papa & cardinales & praelati & clerici, & principes & potentes essent haeretici: & soli simplices & pauperes in fide manerent catholica; . . . aliud non restaret fidelibus quam dolor & gemitus.," ibid., ll. 57-61. "Sicut enim, iuxta promissum Salvatoris, fides catholica est usque ad finem saeculi pérmansura: ita semper erit aliquis in ecclesia, clericus vel laicus, praelatus vel subditus, qui cuicumque errori, qui umquam omnibus fidelibus populis . . . inculcabitur ut credendus, cum instantia forti resistet.," *C. Joann.*, p. 67.

[34]"Christus namque praedicens ecclesiam suam usque ad finem seculi permansuram in fide . . . etiam intelligebat, quod *pro nullo tempore* . . . erat tota ecclesia Christianorum a fide catholica recessura," *Dial.* I, p. 490, ll. 29-33.

[35]Pp. 65-68.

[36]Leff, *William of Ockham*, p. 639, has entirely missed this aspect.

[37]"Quando praelati communiter et populi . . . easdem veritates sub verbis apertis expressas tanquam catholicas expresse vel tacite confitentur. . . . . Hoc autem contingit quandocumque aliquae veritates catholicae per omnes regiones catholicorum publice asseruntur et praedicantur, et apud omnes populos catholicos tanquam catholicae divulgantur et *nullus invenitur catholicus qui tali assertioni resistat,*" p. 67. (Emphasis added.)

[38]One is free to speculate, as does Tierney, *Origins*, p. 236, that the dissenting voice he is thinking of is his own.

[39]"Praemissis autem prelatis & doctoribus in eadem assertione catholici populi consenserunt, quia nullus inventus est populus catholicus qui contradiceret eis ergo haec assertio est universali ecclesiae tribuenda, & per consequens firmiter est tenenda," *Dial.* III, Tr. I, p. 865, ll. 17-20. "Nam fides quam Petrus tenuit . . . nunquam deficiet, sed in aliquibus Christianis clericis vel laicis, viris vel mulieribus, usque ad finem seculi remanebit," *Dial.* I, p. 473, ll. 8-10.

[40]"Si unus solus dissentiret, non esset talis veritas acceptanda," *Dial.* I, p. 429, l. 50.

[41]"In unus solo potest stare tota fides ecclesiae," ibid., l. 51.

[42]"Non est ordo vel unitas [universi] aliquid in re distinctum ab omnibus partibus universi." I *Sent., Ordinatio*, ed. by Badius Ascensius (Lyons: Trechsell, 1495), dist. XXX, q. 1, S. This statement of Ockham's and the treatment of the whole as the sum of its parts must not be construed as a typical "nominalist" denial of the external reality of relationships and of order. Whether or not any so-called "nominalists" make such a denial, Ockham does not, even in philosophy. As Junghans observes, p. 280, if by "nominalism" is meant the denial of a real foundation for the universal concept and the belief that the order of creation is constituted by the understanding only, then Ockham was certainly no nominalist. According to Boehner, *Collected Articles*, p. 163, Ockham certainly accepts an extra-mental order established in things. *A fortiori*, in view of what has been said above, Ockham believes in an order divinely established in the Church which is not just the sum of parts. Cf. Kölmel, *Wilhelm Ockham*, pp. 43, 188, 213-16. Consequently Georges de Lagarde, in the earlier edition of *La naissance*, Vol. V, p. 288, is quite mistaken when he concludes from Ockham's principle that order is not some *thing* distinct from each part of the ensemble that every ensemble can always be reduced to an aggregate of isolated positive things, as though there were no real connections among them, as though everything were only in side-by-side juxtaposition. Lagarde's difficulty seems to be in Ockham's insistence that every existing being is really exterior to every other and that there is really no *participation* of one thing with another in existence. But even without participation there are for Ockham real connections and relationships. In the Church as Ockham sees it, apart from the connections produced by Church structure there is a real connection of all the members in the bond of faith. It is therefore unfortunate that so eminent an ecclesiologist as Congar, *Lay People in the Church* (trans. by Donald Attwater; London: Bloomsbury Publishing Co., 1957), p. 34, can refer to Ockham's theory of the Church as pure nominalist individualism.

[43]Kölmel, *Wilhelm Ockham*, p. 38, points out that Ockham never undertook a real critique of the polarity of absolute singulars and an undoubted order and unity in things.

[44]Pp. 65-66.

[45]*Défense*, p. 152.

[46]*Dial.* I, p. 474, l. 63, p. 475, l. 1; p. 506, ll. 12-14.

[47]Lewis, *Medieval Political Ideas*, Vol. II, pp. 550-51, also describes "Church-rights" as "devolving" upon the faithful remnant. The Latin word translates literally as "devolution," perhaps ambiguous today. The word "devolution"(in verbal or participial forms) is to be found in eight passages of the *Dialogus* and in one passage of the *Octo quaestiones*. Twice Ockham uses it in a purely legal or juridical sense: once of the election of the Roman emperor as possibly devolving (*Dial.* III, Tr. II, p. 899, ll. 44-45), once of the right of calling a general council devolving from recalcitrant dioceses to others (*Dial.* I, p. 603, ll. 26-35, 45-46). Once, in a sense somewhat closer to that above, he uses it of the power of anyone to punish a criminal pope if others fail (*Octo*. Q. I, p. 63). In three places he speaks of a devolvement of the power to judge (*Dial.* I, p. 497, ll. 52-59; ibid., p. 498, ll. 14-18) and to coerce (ibid., p. 626, ll. 45-50) heretics, if all others have fallen into heresy or gravely sinful negligence. Three passages speak of the devolving

again in the case of heresy of all others, of the right to elect the pope (ibid., p. 479, ll. 8-11; p. 502, ll. 52-53). Faith is obviously the *principle* of this devolvement.

⁴⁸"Quilibet in ecclesia militante in manu consilii sui relinquitur, ut secundum suae voluntatis arbitrium manere possit in fide . . . vel a fide catholica deviare: communitas autem Christianorum sic praeservatur a Deo, quod si unus a fide exorbitaverit, alius in fide divino munere permanebit, unde si papa contra fidem erraverit, alius Christianus, vir vel mulier, minime a fide recedet," *Dial.* I, p. 474, l. 63-p. 475, l. 4. Ockham has achieved a possibly undeserved notoriety for suggesting that, if every one else fails in the faith, it would still remain, and the promise of Christ be fulfilled in baptized infants without the use of reason (ibid., p. 506, ll. 40-43). E.g., Lagarde, *Critique*, p. 151, speaks for practically all the modern commentators in accepting this suggestion as Ockham's own opinion. This author is convinced that the opinion is not Ockham's on the basis of the following considerations: a) While in the *Dialogus* the disciple is often represented as fulminating against particular opinions, the Master almost never evaluates them. Yet this position is introduced by the Master saying: "Nescio aliquem Christianum, qui hoc teneat! . . . Ad quaestionem falsam nulla ratio nisi sophistica potest adduci" (p. 506, ll. 2-4). b) However ironic or paradoxical Ockham sometimes appears in the *Dialogus*, he never would say that the reasons he gives for the opinion which is apparently his are "sophistic" or the question "false," and from all one can gather from his total career, he would never admit to himself that his opinion had absolutely no support in Scripture or Tradition. c) All the reasons which are given in support of the position are inconsistent with his often-reiterated principle that though all can deviate from faith, some, or one, will not. A baby *cannot*. d) Everywhere, consistently, he speaks of faith in terms of *acts* of belief, which, of course, infants cannot elicit. To this author the opinion is little more than a dialectical *jeu d'esprit*.

⁴⁹"Quamvis quilibet apostolorum per se a veritate deviare potuerit, sicut & Petrus: tamen collegium apostolorum errare non potuit. Unde & quando Petrus erravit, nequaquam erravit collegium apostolorum, sed unus eorum, scilicet Paulus, ipsum correxit," *Dial.* III, Tr. I, p. 843, ll. 8-12.

⁵⁰"Sicut (iuxta promissionem Christi) fides catholica usque ad finem seculi permanebit: ita in ecclesia Dei potestas de iure coercendi haereticos . . . remanebit, sed si papa cum omnibus clericis esset haereticus, *potestas coercendi de iure haereticos* non esset in papa & in clericis. . . . igitur in isto casu *potestas coercendi haereticos de iure esset ad laicos devoluta*," *Dial.* I, p. 626, ll. 45-49. (Emphasis added.)

⁵¹*Dial.* I, p. 429, l. 51.

⁵²Ibid., p. 451, l. 12; p. 477, ll. 58-59. *Dial.* III, Tr. II, p. 937, ll. 50-51.

⁵³*Dial.* III, Tr. I, p. 828, ll. 19-20: ". . . non frustra esset lex salutis aeterna data Christo, quamvis major pars fidelium imo omnes praeter paucissimos, vel praeter unum errarent."

⁵⁴"Staret enim eadem promissio Christi, si . . . inficerentur omnes praeter duos vel tres," ibid., p. 818, ll. 52-53.

⁵⁵"In uno solo posset consistere, quia propter unum solum posset salvari, etiam quicquid Christus promisit Apostolis," *Dial.* I, p. 451, ll. 12-13.

⁵⁶This Marian theme has been investigated by Congar, "Incidence écclésiologique d'un thème de dévotion Mariale," *Mélanges de science religieuse,* VIII (1950), 277-92.

⁵⁷As McGrade, *Political Thought*, pp. 78-9, also notes. I can partly agree with Miethke, *Ockhams Weg*, pp. 553-54, in his remarks on the restrictive treatment of the exceptional situation. But we have shown throughout this examination how Ockham uses the exceptional situation to relativize the authority of office. But the "special competence" of which Miethke speaks is neither outside the law of the Church's function nor is it in principle or by necessity a rare occurrence.

⁵⁸"*Dis.* Quid si nullus esset sollicitus, ut deberet? *Mag.* Respondetur quod sicut nunquam usque ad finem mundi fides deficiet, ita semper aliquid erit in gratia & debito modo sollicitus de his quae sunt necessaria Dei ecclesiae. Si autem nullus esset sollicitus . . . omnes essent extra gratiam & in peccato mortali, quod nunquam eveniet," *Dial.* III, Tr. II, p. 937, ll. 51-56.

⁵⁹"Quamvis ecclesia universalis . . . non sic possit errare contra fidem nec culpa maculari mortali, ut nullus sit in vera fide et caritate. . . ," *Octo*, Q. VII, p. 177.

[60]*Dial.* III, Tr. II, pp. 872-73.

[61]*Dial.* I, p. 474, l. 60-p. 475, l. 4.

[62]E.g., *C. Joann.*, p. 66. *Dial.* I, p. 400, ll. 50-54. *Dial.* III, Tr. I, p. 864, ll. 55-59.

[63]What is referred to is the Church of the past age *in its historical existence.* Past members of the Church who are now the *ecclesia triumphans* do not enter into the discussion, since Ockham never alludes to their having any *present historical* activity or effect.

[64]I.e., as regards its present historical effect.

[65]*Above*, pp. 68-70.

[66]Introduction, p. 2.

[67]*Harvest*, pp. 361-62.

[68]He does, at least once, speak of what amounts to a tradition "of the holy fathers," but there he is referring to a tradition of Scriptural interpretation: "Scriptura divina est intelligenda sicut a sanctis patribus est exposita," *Dial.* I, p. 489, ll. 59-60. The words are spoken by the disciple, but the master accepts them.

[69]Ibid., p. 410, l. 39-p. 411, l. 52.

[70]"Multae sunt veritates catholicae & fidem sapientes catholicam, quae nec in divinis scripturis habentur explicite: nec ex solis contentis in eis possunt inferri: quibus tamen fidem indubiam explicitam vel implicitam adhibere est necessarium ad salutem," ibid., p. 411, l. 61-p. 412, l. 1.

[71]"Quaedam enim sunt de Deo & Christo secundum humanitatem, ex quibus principaliter salus nostra dependet. . . . Aliae sunt veritates, ex quibus non ita principaliter pendet salus humana: eas tamen oportet firma fide tenere: quia ex revelatione vel approbatione Dei . . . pervenerunt. . . . Nunnullae etiam veritates huiusmodi extra praedictum canonem continentur: quae tamen per revelationem & approbationem divinam mediantibus Apostolis ad catholicos pervenerunt: quia Christus dum viveret in carne mortali cum Apostolis, multa docuit eos . . . quae tamen in Biblia non habentur. . . . Omnes veritates praedictas & quae ex eis consequentia necessaria . . . possunt inferri . . . catholicas esse tenendas. Praeter veritates vero praedictas . . . esse quasdam veritates alias, quae ex solis contentis in Scriptura divina & veritatibus, quae ad nos per Apostolos pervenerunt, concludi non possunt, quae tamen ex praedictis veritatibus, vel aliqua earum & quibusdam aliis veris, quae in facto consistunt, quae vera negari non possunt . . . sequuntur. . . . Adhuc . . . sunt veritatis de gestis ecclesiae & sanctorum," *Dial.* I, p. 412, ll. 3-43, *passim.* It should be especially noted, in terms of Ockham's position relative to the *Scriptura sola* controversy, that while he explicitly speaks of extra-Scriptural truths as objects of belief *de necessitate salutis*, he does not refer specifically to these truths until he comes to deal with the *second* kind of truths he lists here, i.e., those on which our salvation does not primarily depend. Some of these are within, some outside the sacred books. This distinction (principally/non principally) cuts across the distinction of Scriptural/extra-Scriptural sources, but not in such a way as to cover over an important inconsistency. Ockham puts himself in the position both of saying that extra-Scriptural truths are, and of *implying* that they are not necessary for salvation. In the framework of Oberman's categories one could speak of Ockham as an explicit proponent of Tradition II but at heart a man of Tradition I, who regards the Scriptures as the "foundation" of our faith and (implicitly) an adequate account of revelation. See *above*, pp. 101-3.

[72]". . . in Scriptura sacra aut traditionibus Apostolorum aut cronicis historiis vel revelationibus indubitabilibus fidelium, vel his quae sequuntur ex praedictis aut aliquo praedictorum, vel in revelatione seu inspiratione divina modo debito manifesta," *Dial.* I, p. 416, ll. 13-15.

[73]"Primum est earum, quae in Scriptura sacra dicuntur, vel ex eis argumento necessario possunt inferri. Secundum est earum, quae ab Apostolis ad nos per succedentium relationem vel Scripturas fidelium pervenerunt, licet in Scripturis sacris non inveniantur insertae, nec ex solis eis possunt necessario argumento concludi. Tertium est earum, quas in fide dignis cronicis & historiis, relationibus fidelium invenimus. Quartum est earum, quae ex veritatibus primi generis & secundi tantummodo, vel quae ex eis vel alterius earum una cum veritatibus tertii generis possunt manifeste concludi. Quintum est earum, quas Deus praeter veritates revelatas Apostolis

aliis revelavit, vel etiam inspiravit, ac noviter revelaret, vel etiam inspiraret," ibid., p. 415, l. 64-p. 416, l. 7.

[74]Ibid., p. 412, ll. 40-42.

[75]"Ecclesia rite approbando quaecunque in aliquo predictorum generum quinque veritatum se fundavit," ibid., p. 416, ll. 21-22.

[76]Ibid., p. 412, ll. 40-42.

[77]E.g., Thomas Aqqinas, *Summa Theologiae* II-IIae, q. 1, a. 5, *ad secundum, ad tertium*; a. 7, *in corp.*; q. 11, a. 2, *in corp.*

[78]"Est quaedam opinio tenens quod Scripturae divinae contentae in Biblia, & ejusdem sacrae scripturae scriptoribus, & universali eclesiae, atque Apostolis, absque ulla dubitatione in omnibus est credendum," *Dial.* III, Tr. I, p. 821, ll. 28-31.

[79]"Si enim . . . praedicarent contra minimam assertionem scripturae divinae vel doctrinae universalis, non esset eis quoquemodo credendum sed regulae fidei esset firmiter adhaerendum," *Opus, Opera politica*, II, 852-53.

[80]"Ad sacram scripturam et doctrinam seu assertionem universalis ecclesiae oportet recurrere . . . sacra scriptura et doctrina universalis ecclesiae . . . est regula fidei nostrae," *C. Joann.*, p. 72.

[81]*Harvest*, p. 381.

[82]George Tavard, *Holy Writ or Holy Church* (New York: Harper and Brothers, 1959), gives an erroneous presentation of Ockham's doctrine of revelation. He rejects, against the evidence of the text itself, the passages quoted above as not being Ockham's opinion, though he gives no reason for his rejection. Ockham, he says, p. 31, "stands between two extremes that are ably contrasted in his *Dialogue.*" But he gives not a word which would represent a mediating position between the two interpretations of Tradition which he schematizes, p. 22: one tied to Scripture as its living interpretation and the other which makes the Church an independent source of revelation in its tradition. It is true, that Ockham does not free the Church from the teaching of Scripture. But it is equally true that for him there are other sources of revelation within the Church and that "tradition"—a word he almost never uses—could not possibly mean for him only the proper understanding of Scripture. The "doctrine of the universal Church"which Tavard quotes from the *Contra Joannem* (ed. by Scholz, *Streitschriften*, II, 398), is far more than a way in which Ockham "associated Scripture with its interpretation," pp. 30-31.

[83]*C. Bened.*, pp. 245-46.

[84]*Dial.* I, p. 414, ll. 36-42.

[85]"Omnes veritates, quos determinat vel diffinit ecclesia sub aliquo quinque generum praefatorum comprehendi noscuntur. . . . Non est in potestate ecclesiae, quaecunque ad placitum approbare vel etiam reprobare: sed ecclesia rite approbando quaecunque in aliquo praedictorum generum quinque veritatum se fundavit," ibid., p. 416, ll. 15-17, 20-22.

[86]"Tunc quaerendum est an summus pontifex . . . innititur alicui revelationi vel etiam scripturis sacris aut doctrinae ecclesiae universalis; quodcunque istorum detur, sequitur quod summus pontifex per approbationem suam non facit talem veritatem fuisse et esse catholicam," ibid., p. 420, ll. 8-11.

[87]"Nulla veritas est catholica, nisi quia divinitus revelata, vel quia in Scripturis divinis inserta, vel per certitudinem ecclesiae universalis innotuit, vel ex aliquo illorum necessario argumento concluditur. Nihil aut [em] praedictorum ex approbatione summi pontificis vel etiam ecclesiae noscitur dependere," ibid., ll. 14-17.

[88]Van Leeuwen, p. 270, is misled (by not taking this differentiation of statements into account) into thinking that because he reduces the value of defined propositions to their revealed character, Ockham no longer considers the Church the primary rule of faith. Ockham had always denied this status to the *official* institutional Church.

[89]*Above*, ch. i, pp. 32-33.

[90]See *above*, pp. 68-69.

[91]"Hoc non impossibile: quia posset Deus, si sibi placeret, multas veritates catholicas noviter revelare vel inspirare.," *Dial.* I, p. 429, ll. 34-35. He sometimes implies that such is more than mere

possibility: "doctrina quae absque scripturis Apostolicis per revelationem fidelium sibi succedentium vel per scripturas fidelium ad nos pervenit . . . sed etiam illi errores qui alicui veritati post tempora Apostolorum revelatae repugnant. . . ," ibid., p. 422, ll. 41-44. Such passages as the latter, implying that what we would call "tradition" may involve post-Apostolic revelation make nonsense of de Vooght's claim that Ockham worked towards a new synthesis between Scripture and Tradition: "Ainsi l'Écriture et la tradition, tout comme la théologie et l'Écriture, ne font qu'un," Paul de Vooght, *Les sources de la doctrine chrétienne d'après les théologiens du XIVe siècle et du début du XVe* (Paris: Desclée de Brouwer, 1954), p. 245.

[92]See *above*, p. 92.

[93]"Scriptura divina (quae est totius fidei catholicae fundamentum). . . ," *Dial.* I, p. 502, ll. 16-17. ". . . jus autem divinum in scripturis divinis habemus. . . ," *Brev.* Bk. I, ch. iv, p. 45. ". . . in exponendis scripturis et per consequens in traditione seu assertione credendorum. . . ," *C. Bened.*, p. 247.

[94]*Dial.* II, p. 770, ll. 44-45.

[95]Ibid., *Dial.* III, Tr. I, p. 821, l. 34.

[96]". . . cogendo literatiores et intelligentiores eis ut in eorum obsequium intellectum contra rationem et scripturas sacras captivent. . . ," *De imp.*, p. 44.

[97]E.g., "In his quae fidei sunt et scientiae plus me monebit una ratio evidens vel una auctoritas scripturae sacrae sane intelligenda, quam assertio totius universitatis mortalium," ibid., pp. 3-4. "Non diffinierunt [concilia generalia] aliquid nisi quod potest elici ex scripturis divinis," *Dial.* III, Tr. I, p. 826, l. 39. Tierney, *Origins*, offers the suggestive hypothesis that Ockham's polemical purpose for these passages—to limit papal power in temporal affairs—rested entirely on Scripture rightly interpreted. Thus the isolation of Scripture and the aid of reason. (p. 224, n. 1)

[98]"Populus magis credet Scripturae divinae, quam . . . omnibus mortalibus," *Dial.* I, p. 616, ll. 10-12.

[99]"Magis credendum est ecclesia, quae est multitudo catholicorum omnium, quia fuerunt temporibus prophetarum & apostolorum usque modo, quam evangelio: non quia de evangelio sit aliqualiter dubitandum, sed quia totum maius est sua parte. Ecclesia ergo, quae maioris auctoritatis est, quam evangelista, est illa ecclesia, cuius auctor evangelii pars esse dignoscitur," ibid., p. 402, ll. 50-54.

[100]"Haec tota multitudo Christianorum nunc vita mortali viventium non est maioris auctoritatis, quam sit evangelium sanctum," ibid., p. 403, ll. 14-16.

[101]Of course, this correspondence makes sense only in terms of that position on Scripture which we have noted as somewhat inconsistent with his general doctrine of revelation, i.e., that Scripture (as a whole) is the "rule of faith," an adequate presentation of revelation.

[102]"Concors et unanimis approbatio et confessio universalis ecclesiae . . . quae non minoris auctoritatis esse videtur quam . . . etiam auctoritas scripturae divinae. . . ," *C. Joann.*, p. 71.

[103]"Ista enim ecclesia scriptores evangelii & omnes apostolos comprehendit," *Dial.* I, p. 402, l. 46.

3   CONCLUSION

Since at least the time of the Montanist controversy there has been in Western Christianity a tension betwen two different ways of viewing the Church. One way sees the Church principally as the congregation or community of the faithful and thus in terms of its members, whose association in faith is the principal reality of the Church. The other view sees the Church principally as the ensemble of the means of salvation—the "deposit" of faith, the sacraments, ecclesiastical office—and thus a supra-personal institution. In the latter view the institution, founded by Christ, precedes the individual believers, whom it has begotten, and constitutes the primary reality of the Church. In the former, the reality of believing members precedes all else. While both views concern essentials, the historical fact is that they have tended to compete and conflict with each other.

One explanation of the tension between them may be that the religious priorities of the institution, as represented by its officers, are often not the religious priorities of significant numbers of the believers. When the institution was believed to take precedence over the individual believers, as was the case in the High Middle Ages (the orthodox "Catholic" view, according to Congar),[1] the believer generally subordinated himself to the institution. But in the heretical sects of the 12th and 13th centuries the tension appeared openly and extensively. As the institutional Church, at least as regards the papacy, gradually lost in credibility from the late-thirteenth century on, the conflict grew more and more apparent and general.

As a result of his dealing with the Avignon papacy Ockham had certainly experienced a considerable test of his faith in the institutional aspect of the Church. His ecclesiology, in reaction, thus included a much stronger element of Church-as-community than was generally evident in High Medieval ecclesiologies, but because he did not reject the Church as institution it also contained a tension between the two views. In his case, however, the tension is less between institutional and congregational aspects than between two divine laws for the Church. The restrictions, qualifications, and conditions we have noted all amount to a fundamental distinction between the regular and the occasional (exceptional, "casual") functioning of the Church. Office has its divinely constituted place in the regular but not necessarily in the exceptional function. Therefore, there is a double law at work in the Church, a divine institutional law and a divine occasional law.[2] The divine institutional law would encourage and justify the institutional view of the Church, while the

divine occasional law is closely related to the "congregational" view, since the
occasional law is able to detach the official function of the Church from the
institutional office and bestow it non-structurally upon the congregation
(whole or part) or individual.

But there is another difference between Ockham's treatment of the
Church's tensions and traditional attitudes. Heretofore conflict could arise
precisely because institution and congregation, both stemming from Christ,
existed in the same order of divine sanction. They had equal lineage and
inheritance, as it were. For Ockham, in practice if not in theory, they are not
equal. Ockham traces the institution to Christ, but in practice, as we have
seen, because office is open to occasional, non-official intervention and pre-
emption on the part of the congregation, it is always in principle vulnerable to
challenge. Though the authority for such interventions is of divine origin, the
interventions are pursued according to the human judgment of the believer or
believers as to what practical measures are required, as well as how and when
they are to be effected. The authority of office, not being able to prevail
against such interventions, cannot be termed divine without qualification,
unlike "Catholic truths" and the sacraments. At any time the divine will may
operate through the non-official congregation and subject Church authority
to the faith-prerogatives and practical decisions of the believers. The effect is
to detach office and structure from the unconditional divine reality of the
Church. Church office is not "divine" in the way faith and sacraments are,
since his acknowledgment of its divine authority is more verbal than real.

Ockham does not appear to face up to this lack of coherence in his
ecclesiolog, a Church divinely instituted in its faith, fellowship, offices, and
sacraments, and yet having a divine guarantee which ignores the institution
itself. However non-problematic such a view will come to seem after the
Reformation, it was a strange one indeed for a medieval theologian claiming
to be orthodox, a view which departs from the very strong consensus of ten or
eleven centuries of Christian thinking about the Church. How would he
explain the isolation of one divinely-instituted element from the others? On
what theoretical grounds would he justify his alienation of the structure of the
Church from the Church's inner reality and essential function, when the same
Lord has given both? He does not say; and the apparent reason is that he did
not see this alienation either as fact or as problem.

It is true that any generalizations about Ockham's ecclesiology must
remain somewhat tentative in view of the occasional, non-systematic and
polemical character of his ecclesiological writings, but that very character
perhaps tells us something. In a polemically charged atmosphere he should
have regarded so untraditional an alienation as an obvious challenge to
received notions, which required justification and defense. That Ockham
omitted such a defense would seem to suggest that he had not noticed his
having taken away with one hand what he had given with the other: that he
had presented divine institution without divine *guarantee*. If his opponents

noticed it they have not singled it out, probably regarding that particular alienation as the least of his offenses.

Ockham appears never to have seen the incompatibility inherent in his acceptance of the structured-hierarchical institution of the Church by Christ and his treatment of the Church as faith-communion. For him the Church is a society at once divine and human—not, as in more traditional medieval views, divine in institution and means, human in membership—but both divine and human in institutional means also. It is not true that this view of the Church separates the visible from the invisible elements, as though only the invisible were the true Church.[3] The Church for him is the visible kingdom of Christ,[4] and there is no separation of visible from invisible elements in the regular functioning of the Church. Even when the prerogatives of true faith must operate apart from or contrary to the regular institutional function, they have external and quite visible effects. True believers can summon the Church to a council; the college of cardinals—or any body of believers to whom the responsibility may devolve—may decide to elect no pope for a time: the clergy and people of Rome may depose their pontiff, etc. All of these are external, social actions with quite visible, social consequences. True belief here is wedded to the visible, social elements of 'political' action and even structural change. There is to be no separation between visible and invisible, and no allocation of the reality of the Church strictly to the invisible functioning of faith. Ockham does not present two forms of the Church, but rather two laws for the Church, both intended to be taken as divine. There is the normative, regular law of the institution and the higher law of faith which authorizes the occasional or emergency intervention. But while the true Faith and the fellowship created by it are unconditional divine realities, the institutional office is not. There is thus an alternating of divine laws for the Church which divides its authority and which in practice could hardly avoid surrendering the Church to the struggle of competing claims. This division—a division which is not seen as disrupting the unity of the Church but as occurring within it— characterizes Ockham's ecclesiology more than does the tension between institutional means and congregation.

How then does Ockham arrive at this view of the Church? At the outset he appears to have seen the problem as one of holding together his belief in the indefectibility of faith in the Church and the fact that the highest authority of the Church was in heresy. He saw the necessity of relating the prayer and promise of Christ to a Church viewed in dissociation from its hierarchical structure. He had to view the reality of the Church, that is, its very nature, in a new way. Christ's prayer and promise must concern the Church's true nature and object and this must be separable from the traditional structures. During the course of this study we have repeated again and again: "The Church *as object* of prayer and promise. . . ." This has not been done to indicate that Ockham merely insisted on one particular aspect of the Church's nature and life, but to show that for him what Christ prayed for and promised must have been what the Church is really all about. And this, he concluded, is to be a congregation called together by God for true belief, a congregation of believers. All else in the Church's reality—divinely instituted office and even the divinely efficacious sacraments—is of secondary value.

At this point it would seem that he faced two principal tasks. The first was to show how the inner nature of the Church could be disengaged from its structures, while at the same time acknowledging the divine validity of those structures. The second was to find a view of the totality of the Church which would at once justify the efficacy of prayer and promise and show how the Church could be a congregation of true believers.

The first task consists in showing how something which was divinely instituted is nevertheless not of absolute and unquestionable, but rather of relative and conditional value. Ockham's efforts here were ingenious, if as we have said, ultimately unsuccessful. To meet this challenge he adopted the strategy of setting the divinely-given values of the institution into the wider context of other values, also divinely-given. God, who in Christ gave us the institution of the Church, also gave us the immutable divine law, the light of reason, which must decide some matters even of divine law, the Gospel of Christian freedom, and most of all Revelation itself, which must reign supreme over the Church and all its officers. Employing this strategy, Ockham did not need to challenge or deny the divine authorization of the Church structure; he had only to set out the larger context in which the limitations of official prerogatives would, he thought, be clear. No one would be disposed to doubt that the divine law is to be preferred to human law; and Church authority, though authorized by Christ himself, can issue only human law. The pope may have authority from Christ, but the people of Rome have, by natural law (which is really divine law), the right in given circumstances to depose him. (This right can of course devolve to the emperor, who, though a lay leader, is a member of the Roman Church.) The papacy may have been directly instituted by Christ, but the Church as a whole may always use its rational discretion—for reason, too, is from God—to judge whether or not at any time the filling of the papal office is opportune for the interests of faith. At certain times reason may judge that a plurality of popes is either opportune or unavoidable.

By the broad range he assigns to the discretion of reason—it presides over all matters except faith and the immutable commands of the divine law— Ockham establishes the relativity of all human arrangements and the rule of reason not only in human affairs, but even the affairs of the Church. The will of Christ establishes the rule of reason in the constitution of the Church.[5]

While never setting out an explicit hierarchy of values, Ockham continually rises from the consideration of authority in the Church and even from its constitution to the discussion of the natural and divine laws, where the will of Christ for the Church is more broadly expressed. Ultimately and most properly, appeal is made to the needs of faith (although these are determined by reason). Most important among the restrictions of Church authority are those which are imposed by the nature of the Gospel, which is for Christians a law of liberty. Christian liberty demands that Church authority, even as vested in the pope, not command anything beyond the scope of the decalogue, since the Gospel does not so command. Within this scope no Christian is to be commanded in the ordinary course to any work which is only of counsel or of supererogation. The freedom of the Gospel is above papal law.

Ockham's sincerity in desiring only to limit institutional authority and not negate it does not really need to be questioned.[6] But the result of all his relativizations and qualifications is to make Church authority and structure appear in a novel light, strange to more traditional Medieval theologies. The Church of Ockham has been "de-politicized," its authority and function spiritualized.

The mark of this spiritualization is that the ultimate rule for the Church's order as well as its faith is that of Revelation itself—"Scripture and the doctrine of the universal Church." Since the latter have been given by God as the true Faith, it is faith which is the nature and purpose of membership in the Church. By faith we belong to a fellowship in Christ. True belief appears to constitute for Ockham the common good of the Church and its real nature, which is ultimately only to be a faith-community; and while he does not explicitly say that everything else in the Church, even its sacraments, exists only for the good of true believing, he does in fact subordinate everything else to the needs of faith. He may say that the Church is a visible kingdom, but its only true bond is the invisible union of faith.

The Church is essentially a faith-community because the prayer and promise of Christ—which must have been directed to the essence of the Church—were directed to the faith of its members. How then can the Church in its totality be the community of true believers? Ockham's second task was to explain this.

His problem here is obvious. In the first place, the Church could not be the community of true believers as a hierarchically structured society: the pope, the college of cardinals, the whole Avignon curia, numerous prelates and religious superiors were heretics, having denied evangelical poverty. The Church must be that community of true believers apart from its structures, and at times in spite of them. Is the Church that community as an aggregate whole? This, too, cannot be, since countless believers of past and present, besides those already mentioned, have lapsed from the true faith. There must be a way of viewing the community of those addressed by Christ which will allow that the faith promised will always exist in and for that community as a whole, if not in all its members.

That view of the Church as a totality of believers which Ockham forged in answer to his needs we have called the cumulative-distributive view of the Church. By seeing the faith of the Church as a cumulative reality (in its tradition and as a single, historical object of the divine will) and at the same time as a reality distributed among its members, who separately can carry its prerogatives, Ockham tried to account for prayer and promise. But he seems never to have seen that his treatment is ambiguous. Prayer and promise are given to all and yet not to all. They are given to the whole Church and to no part, and yet may sometimes be realized in a single individual. The ambiguity can be precisely located in the question of who really are the object of prayer and promise: the whole congregation or the true believers. In the cumulative treatment Ockham's answer is: the whole congregation (and no part). In the distributive treatment it is: the true believers (even if they are few or one). Thus he never consistently interpreted prayer and promise.

Ambiguous too is his treatment of the cumulative reality of the Church as object of prayer and promise. The latter must be directed to a determinate object: they must function in the order of reality. As soon as they do, a distribution takes effect; the whole is actually always a distributed, never a cumulative, reality. The accumulation has been a merely mental act all along, although Ockham has spoken of it as though it were real. It is ironic that he, especially, should shift ambiguously between the real and the mental orders. The reality of the cumulative whole is not saved by seeing it as tradition or as the completed object of prayer and promise in the mind of God. Tradition as such is only the record of individual acts of belief; the terrestrial Church of all times exists in the real order only as distributed. But since the innermost unity of the Church is one of faith, if the cumulative whole of believers is not a real unity, *the Church has no unity*.

Thus the cumulative-distributive view does not really solve the problem. The "you" of Christ's prayer and promise must be interpreted as *either one or many*, and the cumulative whole is not one because it is not real. (Even the Church of any one age is not a cumulative reality in terms of the function of prayer and promise. One believer alone may have the true faith.) The "you" which is of course a multitude of persons, lacking as it does unanimity of faith, can be one not cumulatively but only as any multitude of persons is one: in terms of some kind of societal structure. Thus, whether he realized it or not, Ockham was faced with a dilemma. If prayer and promise were given to the Church as a unity, they were given to the Church living its historical life as *this* hierarchical institution and have thus been voided. If they were not given to the Church as structured they have no determinate, unified object and thus the Church as *congregation* of believers is not one.

Thus Ockham has left his interpretation of prayer and promise radically ambiguous: the Church as a unity is irreconcilable with the Church as a distributive reality, but Ockham's interpretation of prayer and promise involves both. In this perspective it can be seen that the whole business of devolvement is nothing more than a strategy to create a *functional* unity flowing from true belief where actually there is none. Ockham wants a real, functioning unity of faith without structure, but he cannot have it. Ockham's

Church is finally no definable, tangible socio-historical entity. An invisibly shifting number of believers with fundamentally indeterminable arrangements of authority and responsibility do not a Church make, in any empirically understandable sense of the word, certainly from the point of view of the believer of that time.

It was stated at the outset of this investigation that the attempt would be made to determine whether Ockham had an ecclesiology which was specific, distinctive, and coherent. It should be clear at this point that Ockham's cumulative-distributive treatment of the Church-whole is persistent and pervasive enough to merit being considered specific to him. He has, that is, a particular ecclesiological view. And until it can be shown that such a view, with its accompanying relativizations, can be found elsewhere in late-medieval ecclesiological thinking not influenced by him, his ecclesiology deserves to be considered distinctive as well. What it cannot be called, as we have seen, is *coherent*.

Ockham's atentuation of the validity of the structure of the Church, which underlies his ambiguous interpretation of Christ's prayer and promise, has left his ecclesiology hopelessly stranded. The Church is a faith-community but it cannot function institutionally with complete divine sanction; its life is faith, but that faith has no unity of subjects as it is no unified object of prayer and promise. That which can actually and effectually function in the Church is human and radically questionable: that which is divine in the Church cannot effectually and visibly function. Ockham holds to his faith that the Church is a divine work, the work of Christ. He is, however, unable to describe that work and so his ecclesiology is not ultimately viable. The step he would not take to make it viable, the denial of the divine institution of the hierarchical structure of the Church and thus of a divinely-given visible unity, was to be taken by the sixteenth-century Reformers.

What are we to say about the Occamist ecclesiology as it relates to what went before and what came after? It is indeed a transitional conception, and the tensions within it are precisely those between the conceptions of earlier times and those which were to come after. With the "high" ecclesiologies of the thirteenth-fourteenth-century curialists, he sees the Church as the divinely-institutionalized system of sacramental grace and hierarchical office of teaching and ruling, culminating in the supreme pontiff. In anticipation of Reformation ecclesiologies he sees the sharing of faith as fundamental to the Church, called into being by the Word of God. By faith God reigns directly and supremely, never surrendering His dominion to structure and office. With the High Middle Ages Ockham considers the hierarchical Church an institution of divine foundation; with the Reformers he denies ultimate divine sanction to the papacy, to a general council, or to any Church office.

The Church of Ockham is no longer that of Aquinas because it no longer has a unifying principle which adequately accounts for all the divinely-instituted phenomena. Even the unity of true believers is, as we have seen, no true unity. There is no subsistent unity in the Church, the only accidental unity being the concordance in faith shared by those members who happen to believe the objectively true Faith. Perhaps Ockham's most striking departure from the ecclesiology of the thirteenth century is the disjunction he introduces between divine and human authority in the Church. The authority insofar as it is actually at their disposal, wielded by human beings, is never divine but always only human. The "vicar of Christ" in the papal office is for Ockham Christ's vicar in a sense vastly diminished from that which Aquinas held. The assymetry between the structure of the Church and its inner nature seems clear evidence of his general conception of the discontinuity between the human and divine spheres of being. The omnipotent freedom of God entails that He infinitely transcend the grasp of the Church, and since the members of the Church belong only to Him, *they* transcend the grasp and management of the Church's structure and of anything other than the demands of faith.

Here, it seems to this writer, one can see the justification for the opinion of Boehner that there are "inner connections" between Ockham's philosophy and his church-political thinking, as well as Kölmel's explanation that they are related ways of seeing.[7] But it is also clear that Ockham could easily have felt himself driven to his ecclesiology by a coming together of purely theological and orthodox considerations about the divine promises, the divine institution of the hierarchical Church-structure, and received notions about the poverty of Christ. In other words, he need not have consulted any of his philosophical tenets to arrive at his ecclesiology; but in arriving there he appears to have found it useful as well as natural to see the relationship of God to the Church much as he saw the relationship of faith to reason and to view the order of the Church as conditioned and contingent in much the way he saw order in the ordered parts of any *universum* as a contingent fact. More than this sort of relationship, it seems to me, ought not to be claimed for the connection between Ockham's ecclesiology and his philosophy.

As it is no longer the Church of Aquinas, Ockham's Church is not yet that of Luther. The difference is not only a different conception of saving faith or of such specifics as the place of Scripture in the Church, etc. Ockham still believes in that form of the ecclesiastical institution presented by the hierarchical Church of his day. If he has diminished its authorization irreversibly he has not yet accepted the consequences of what he has done, nor has he seen what the next steps would be. He disavowed the radicalism of Marsilius, who allowed the structure of the Church no more than the moral authority of suasion, who denied not only the primacy of the papal office but the divine institution of the episcopacy itself. And if he rejected Marsilius' affirmation of the authority and infallibility of the general council, he rejected as well his teaching of the sole sufficiency of Scripture.

While it has to be admitted that the effort was not finally successful, Ockham strove for a position intermediate between the authoritarianism and structural absolutism of the curialist ecclesiologies of thirteenth and fourteenth centuries and the rejection of ecclesiastical Christianity implied by some of the radicals of his time. Perhaps because his Church-thinking has no ultimate coherence its main lines were not pursued in succeeding generations. His disengaging of structure from spiritual prerogative could indeed have provided a precedent for Wyclif's rejection of ecclesial authority not rooted in grace. His doctrine of an emergency transfer (devolvement) of authority to the community of the Church according to the needs of the situation was certainly taken up by the conciliarists and used in arriving at their tenet that ultimate authority resides in the Church as a whole, but as Tierney has shown, where he departed from the canonists the conciliarists departed from him.[8] The line thus traceable from Ockham's devolvement to later ecclesiologies manifests certain definite continuities, theoretical if not historical, but more can scarcely be claimed for the enduring influence of Ockham's conception of the Church.

It takes its place in the movement which had surfaced with John of Paris among sober and orthodox theologians at the turn of the fourteenth century, a movement away from the narrowly institutional toward a more "evangelical" conception of Church, which sought its spirit and sanction more directly in New Testament teaching, a conception which was to be consummated in the Reformation ecclesiologies. It took shape at a time when Christians were trying to hold to traditional views without any longer being able to accept the view of reality and truth which undergirded them. The intolerable tensions and ultimate contradictions to be found in Ockham's treatment of the Church are part of the general testimony of those times to the futility of trying to put new wine into old wineskins. They are perhaps not more characteristic of Ockham's thought than they are of the uncertain and groping spirit of the late medieval world.

---

[1] *Lay People in the Church*, p. 25.

[2] These two laws in no way correspond, as Köhler would have it, to the distinction Ockham makes between the *potentia ordinata* and the *potentia absoluta* in God, pp. 44, 66, 74. Both laws are already ordained for the Church in the divine will. They do testify to Ockham's constant interest in the dialectic between fact and possibility in a contingent world, of which he sees the institutional Church as inextricably a part. As McGrade has pointed out, *The Political Thought of William of Ockham*, p. 78, a "balanced dualism" involving the alternation of "regular"and "casual" power in both political and ecclesiastical life is Ockham's way of seeing the functioning of all lawful social order.

[3] Köhler persists in this misunderstanding, e.g., pp. 49, 54.

[4] *Opus, Opera politica*, II, p. 680.

[5] E.g., see *Opus, Opera politica*, II, p. 582. *Octo*, Q. I, p. 62. *Dial*. I, p. 654, ll. 7-15.

[6] As Tierney gratuitously does, *Origins*, pp. 235-36.

[7] See *above*, Intro. n. 1.

[8] Tierney, "Ockham, the Conciliar Theory, and the Canonists," *Journal of the History of Ideas*, IV (1954), 49-62.